THE AUTHOR

L. Craig Parker, Jr., is at present Professor of Criminal Justice at the University of New Haven. He received his AB degree in Psychological Services from Springfield College. Prior to being awarded his PhD from the State University of New York at Buffalo, he worked as a counselor in a federal pre-release guidance center for youthful offenders and as a clinical psychologist for the New York State Department of Mental Hygiene. In 1967 he was appointed Assistant Professor at the University of Wisconsin, where he taught rehabilitation counseling and criminal justice. In 1970, he joined the faculty of the University of Alberta as an Associate Professor and Counseling Psychologist. During that period, he provided in-service training for the Royal Canadian Mounted Police and the Edmonton City Police Department. His publications include *Legal Psychology* (Charles Thomas, 1980), and, with R.D. Meier, *Interpersonal Psychology for Law Enforcement and Correction* (West Publishing Company, 1980), as well as numerous articles for journals and magazines.

L. Craig Parker, Jr.

THE JAPANESE POLICE SYSTEM TODAY

An American Perspective

KODANSHA INTERNATIONAL
Tokyo and New York

Jacket photo: Courtesy of the National Police Agency.

Distributed in the United States by Kodansha International/USA, Ltd., through Harper & Row, Publishers, Inc., 10 East 53rd Street, New York, New York 10022. Published by Kodansha International Ltd., 2-2, Otowa 1-chome, Bunkyo-ku, Tokyo 112 and Kodansha International/USA, Ltd., 10 East 53rd Street, New York, New York 10022. Copyright in Japan 1984 by Kodansha International Ltd. All rights reserved. Printed in Japan.
LCC 83-48877
ISBN 0-87011-853-6
ISBN 4-7700-1353-1 (in Japan)
First edition, 1984
First paperback edition, 1987

To Isshu Takahashi,
my friend and colleague,
who inspired
my interest in Japan.

CONTENTS

PREFACE

I anticipated an interesting year in Japan when I was informed that I had received a Fulbright Research Fellowship for 1980–81, but I had no idea that my plan to study police–community relations would turn out to be such a challenging and rewarding experience. At the outset, less than twenty-four hours after my arrival in Tokyo, I was informed that the National Police Agency could give me "about one week in September" for my research. However, soon after this news, which had been relayed by the Ministry of Foreign Affairs to the Fulbright office, I had the good fortune to meet a prestigious Japanese legal scholar who immediately contacted two members of the Tokyo Public Safety Commission and set in motion a series of introductions that proved invaluable in my efforts to gain support for my research program.

As I learned quickly, without personal introductions many projects are doomed in Japan. This problem is not peculiar to foreigners: the Japanese face it as well. A Japanese businessman will not approach a fellow businessman or a bureaucrat without proper introduction if he expects to be successful in his endeavors. Often the initiating party will go through a former classmate or use an acquaintance in arranging the meeting. This "go-between" may be able to lay the groundwork or actually arrange an introduction. The Japanese have a word for this: *nemawashi*, "to lay the groundwork for obtaining one's objective." I was fortunate that despite the initial unresponsiveness of the police bureaucracy, with some timely *nemawashi* I was able to obtain their full cooperation. Once they agreed to help, I was denied nothing.

Over the last ten years or so, two other Western researchers have penetrated the Japanese police bureaucracy and have conducted extensive studies (see David H. Bayley, *Forces of Order: Police Behavior in Japan and the United States*, Berkeley and Los Angeles: University of California Press, 1976, and Walter L. Ames, *Police and Community in Japan*, Berkeley and Los Angeles: University of California Press, 1981). Despite the fact that these studies convey a complimentary view of Japanese police services, conversations I have had with legal scholars and officials have convinced me that the police are reluctant to accommodate further research. One may ask, however, whether there is a police agency anywhere in the world that is eager to receive researchers. By the very nature of police work, administrators shy away from exposing the inner mechanisms of their agencies. However, in this instance there may have been an advantage to being an outsider. A legal scholar at Sophia University in Tokyo pointed out that just as it might be easier for a Japanese researcher to gain access to the police community in America, likewise a Japanese police department might be more willing to receive a foreign official or scholar than his Japanese counterpart.

There are advantages to approaching a country with an open mind, free from bias and preconceived notions, but I must admit that on more than one occasion I would have gladly traded my newcomer status for that of a seasoned scholar familiar with the language and customs of Japan. Not being a "Japanologist" placed a burden on me as a researcher, but my Japanese friends and colleagues were invaluable in assisting me in getting acquainted with the country and its customs. Fellow scholars and criminal justice professionals were particularly helpful; I felt that there were any number of them upon whom I could rely for assistance.

On the other hand, there were many occasions when my status as a newcomer worked to my advantage. For the uninitiated foreigner the simplest daily encounter can be a learning experience, whether it be asking directions—in which police are frequently very helpful—or trying to get on the right subway for Shinjuku.

Occasionally my requests for assistance from an ordinary citizen on a mundane matter, such as locating the proper train in a busy subway station, would go unheeded, but my Japanese friends pointed out that frequently this was because of the embarrassment that some Japanese feel because of their inability to answer in English. Since English is taught beginning in junior high school, there is an expectation that most Japanese are able to speak at least a little. The inability to do so in such a situation is usually due to a lack of self-confidence. In the majority of cases, however, I encountered a willingness to help, and indeed many times Japanese people went out of their way to assist me.

My research relied on a participant observation approach. I conducted five months of investigation in Tokyo, two months in Hokkaido, and an additional month in a variety of other locations throughout Japan. I made numerous visits to police boxes and conducted many interviews with police officers, public prosecutors, social scientists, legal scholars, judges, probation officers, and citizens. I was able to cross-check sensitive information that emerged from the field study of police behavior with individual police officers and scholars who became my friends. My twelve years' background in professional consulting and teaching police in North America also provided a valuable framework for evaluating observations of the Japanese system.

For the most part I found the police to be candid and forthright. Japanese officials are naturally interested in making a favorable impression, so one is usually treated with respect at police boxes. This is preferable to having to contend with hostility or total indifference, but this politeness, for which the Japanese are known, can also be a hindrance to the researcher. It is necessary for the foreigner to have associates he can rely upon and with whom he can cross-check matters such as the disciplining of officers and weaknesses within the system. In the United States, precinct-level police might or might not cooperate with a researcher regardless of whether or not he had the support of the police administration. In Japan, once the police administration agrees to assist you, there is full compliance at all levels. This is just one example of the vertical hierarchical structure of Japanese society that Chie

Nakane described so accurately. As in the Japanese industrial sector, teamwork and support are very much in evidence among the police. Loyalty is also highly valued and commands from superiors are typically executed to the letter by lower-ranking officers. In the United States, a research project involving street-level police personnel would need the approval of both the administration and union leadership, while in Japan no such complication arises. Moreover, a job action by sick calls, such as the "blue flu" that afflicted Chicago police a few years ago, would be unimaginable in Japan. Japanese police are not unionized.

Several people were particularly helpful, and I would like to take this opportunity to thank them. My friend and colleague, Isshu Takahashi, a law professor at Hosei University, was of immeasurable assistance in familiarizing me with Japanese customs and behavior. My biggest handicap was my inability to speak Japanese, and I was extremely fortunate in being able to obtain the services of such a bright and versatile translator as Mari Kurihara, who played a critical role in helping me cope with the language problem. She is the daughter of a Japanese diplomat and has traveled widely during her twenty-six years. She graduated from Keio University and speaks excellent English. Her extensive exposure to Western culture allowed her to be sensitive to my research concerns. As a friend noted, an interpreter does much more than change English phrases into Japanese ones and vice versa: she or he also acts as an intermediary between the researcher and the subjects of the study. Mari Kurihara was able to relate to police officers and other officials in a candid, friendly manner, which greatly facilitated my dialogue with them. With her family background and experience, she was at ease with high-ranking officials as well as with working police. In the Japanese language, knowing the appropriate level of politeness to use in a given situation is essential. Mari Kurihara was able to aid me in interpreting the various nuances of interpersonal relationships expressed in the language itself.

While initially I had been concerned about using a female interpreter in Japan's masculine police world, I came to realize that the sex of the interpreter was far less important than the personality of the individual. I consulted any number of Japanese colleagues on this subject and the general consensus was that a well-qualified woman interpreter would be perfectly acceptable. Since interpreters tend to be women in Japan, I believe there was nothing unusual in an American professor arriving at a police box accompanied by a woman interpreter.

I would be remiss were I not to mention the fine assistance offered by Susumu Kitaidai, a twenty-three-year-old former student at International Christian University. Kitaidai is fluent in English. Like Mari Kurihara he had spent a number of years outside of Japan. He had, in fact, lived almost half his life in White Plains, New York and Washington, D.C. Periodically he filled in for Mari Kurihara when she was not available.

During the period of my research in Japan many people assisted me by arranging contacts, offering suggestions, and gathering data. I could not hope to list all of them, but they include Mitsuo Uehara, Ryuichi Hirano, Minoru Shikita, Nobushige Ukai, Yasuhiro Okudaira, Yoshiaki Takahashi, Haruo Nishimura, Shingo Suzuki, Senior Superintendent Teragaki, Shinichi Tsuchiya, Eisau Sato, Keizo Hagihara, Saku Machino, Yozo Yokota, Yoshiyuki Matsumura, Hiroshi Nakazawa, Ken Hattori, Mutsumi Nakahara and Tamiyo Togasaki. The Fulbright Office and Caroline Yang provided much-needed encouragement and support.

Also, I wish to thank the following persons for reading the manuscript and offering helpful criticisms and comments: Nancy Taylor, Michael Young, Eleanor Westney, Tsuyoshi Kinoshita, Kanehiro Hoshino, Toichi Fujiwara, Eitetsu Yamaguchi, and Kimberly Till. Lawrence and Virginia Parker helped in the preparation of the manuscript, though any remaining difficulties of form or content are, of course, my responsibility.

L. CRAIG PARKER
Professor of Criminal Justice
University of New Haven
September 1983

Chapter 1

OVERVIEW: CRIME IN JAPAN AND THE UNITED STATES

Awareness of Japan in the United States has increased rapidly in the past decade, largely due to what is perceived as a growing economic threat. With the economic anxiety, however, has come a certain amount of cross-cultural curiosity. Among the points of interest is Japan's surprisingly low crime rate. Though less dazzling than the economic achievements of "Japan Inc.," facts such as the lack of crime are beginning to draw our attention to a national phenomenon that is far more complex and, I feel, far more interesting than the simple ability to produce good, small cars.

For eight months in 1980–81, I strolled on the streets of Tokyo, Kyoto, Yokohama, Kobe, Sapporo, and a number of other Japanese cities and towns without once feeling threatened or menaced by an individual or a group. I rode subways that were not defaced with graffiti, and I wandered through parks at midnight in the heart of Tokyo without apprehension. I concede that this state of mind took a while to acquire, since I was accustomed to the streets of New York and Boston before arriving in Tokyo. Though not altogether crime-free, by any yardstick one wishes to use Japan is a country that continues to have a relatively tranquil and safe social environment. This is a remarkable feature of Japanese society that deserves attention from the United States, which is in the midst of a crime crisis. One way to illustrate the success of the Japanese in this area is by comparison with the United States, and while this work is not intended to be a systematic, point by point comparison of each country's approach to law enforcement, I would like to begin with a comparative perspective. The primary purpose of this book, however, is to explore the role of the police in community relations in Japan, as seen through the eyes of a psychologist.

Comparisons are difficult to draw between crime data reported in Japan and the United States because the different levels of confidence in police effectiveness in these countries result in different rates of reporting crime. In addition, descriptive terms for crimes —even after making allowances for the inaccuracy of translation —may have different connotations in each country, further confounding comparisons.

It appears that the Japanese report a larger percentage of crime than Americans do. This is evidenced by the discrepancies between their various crime indices and our own. Because of the unreliability of statistical data issued in the *Uniform Crime Reports* of the F.B.I., the U.S. Department of Justice began direct household surveys of crime a number of years ago. This approach revealed, not surprisingly, a significantly higher incidence of actual crime than that reported by citizens to police.

The F.B.I., as the clearinghouse or coordinating agency, must contend not only with the outright manipulation of data as reported by many police departments but also with varying systems of crime classification. Admittedly, there is an attempt to have police from different cities standardize reporting of crime, but this appears to have enjoyed only modest success. Pressure to report certain types of crime has political implications for local police chiefs. A police analyst eager to obtain federal funds for a pet project may "stack the deck" in a certain category. Thus, ultimately, the F.B.I. must rely on the veracity of the reports issued by the hundreds of police agencies throughout the nation, even though error and bias are known to exist.

The National Police Agency in Japan coordinates policy making and standards for the forty-seven prefectural police organizations throughout the country and thus has an advantage when it comes to the standardization of police practices and the compilation of data. The reporting system and classification of crime data are therefore more accurate. Since high-ranking police officials are more insulated from the whims of local politicians and since they are rotated in their assignments approximately every two years, they are much less vulnerable to pressures to tamper with the raw data in their possession. This subject will be discussed later in more detail.

Notwithstanding the problems inherent in reporting and compiling statistical data, what do some of the comparisons between Japan and other nations indicate for a recent year? The Japanese *White Paper on Crime, 1980* (Ministry of Justice, 1980) reports the following incidence of homicide for various cities around the world during 1978 (per 100,000 population): New York, 20.1; Chicago, 25.4; London, 4.2; Paris, 6.8; Tokyo (Metropolitan), 2.0. H. Scott-Stokes reported that in Tokyo during 1980, "There was only one case of a burglar breaking and entering a home and killing someone inside." He added, "There was not one murder during a robbery attempt on the streets, in the parks, or in the subways."[1] The *White Paper* statistics on robbery are: New York, 989.4; Paris, 479.1; and Tokyo (Metropolitan), 4.4. Finally, if one looks at the problem of theft, equally impressive information is offered: New York, 5,983.3; Chicago, 5,263.9; London, 6,254.0; Paris, 8,079.1; and Tokyo (Metropolitan), 1,905.2. With the exception of theft, the largest discrepancies in identified crime are consistently between New York and Tokyo. Thus, New York (population 7.5 million) has ten times as many murders as Tokyo (population 8.3 million) and a shocking two hundred and twenty-five times as many robberies. (European cities do not have the glaringly high crime rates of major American cities, but even in comparison to them, Japanese cities still have impressively low crime rates.) A more comprehensive comparison is offered in Table 1. How can this be accounted for, considering the fact that Japan's population is as urbanized, industrialized, and sophisticated as the most advanced Western nations? This is not a matter that is elusive and defies understanding. Moreover, by understanding it, it is possible for us to gain a greater appreciation of our own crime problems.

For years, the Japanese seemed to accept without question the

Table 1
International Comparison of Crime
(1978; per 100,000 population)

Country/City	Homicide	Robbery	Injury	Theft	Rape
U.S.A.	9.0	191.3	255.9	4,622.4	30.8
New York	20.1	989.4	578.3	5,983.3	51.9
Chicago	25.4	491.5	333.2	5,263.9	43.3
Los Angeles	23.9	627.2	607.8	7,207.4	90.5
U.K.	2.0	26.8	173.1	3,989.1	10.1
London	4.2	93.8	196.7	6,254.0	6.4
France	3.5	55.1	57.9	2,469.4	3.1
Paris	6.8	479.1	168.4	8,079.1	6.8
F.R.G	4.1	35.3	85.4	3,613.5	10.8
West Berlin	6.4	119.3	234.3	6,837.6	26.2
Hamburg	4.7	91.7	144.4	6,658.4	19.4
Japan	1.6	1.7	25.1	986.9	2.5
Tokyo (Metro)	2.0	4.4	45.2	1,905.2	3.6
Yokohama	2.2	2.2	36.7	948.0	2.9
Osaka	4.0	3.3	49.6	1,993.9	2.5

Source: Ministry of Justice, 1980.

difference between their society and others' on the subject of crime control. Recently, however, the publication of various books by Bayley, Ames, and Clifford has helped to awaken Westerners to what is occurring in the Japanese system of justice, and in turn the Japanese have become more conscious of their own success. Some discussion of the Japanese approach to crime appeared in Vogel's best-selling book *Japan as Number One*, but his work addressed business, education, government, and social welfare practices as well. Thus, the treatment of crime and justice was necessarily cursory. Nonetheless, his book reached a wide audience and contributed to the growing awareness that Japan enjoys a relatively crime-free society.

Alvin Toffler, the author of *Future Shock*, collaborated with his wife, Heidi, on a series of articles that focused on the strengths and weaknesses of Japanese society. The Tofflers expressed concern that the media bombardment of the early eighties, which emphasized Japanese successes, would result in a "backlash." In their view, a caricature has been emerging in which "we see 115,000,000 docile, dedicated and highly motivated workers smoothly managed by a few giant, paternalistic corporations whose top leaders work hand-in-glove with an understanding government."[2] In their opinion, this picture is far from the truth. The notion of "No. 1" grossly oversimplifies a nation that has real weaknesses and vulnerabilities in addition to its highly advertised strengths. As one example, they cite Japan's energy problems. While in the United States we rely upon other nations for just 22.4 percent of our energy requirements, Japan must import 86.3 percent of its energy. Concerning food supplies, the Tofflers remind us that while Americans are among the top food exporters in the world, the EEC must import 25 percent of its food and the Japanese are required to import over 50 percent to meet demand. In short, while Japanese fuel-efficient automobiles, technologically sophisticated radios and television sets, and other quality products are attracting wide attention, a fragility exists in some aspects of Japanese life that should not be ignored by those who are intent on creating the myth of a "superstate."

The issues related to the low crime rate in Japan that will be explored in this book include the following: first, the homogeneous makeup of Japanese society, which is a powerful factor in exerting social controls on illegal, and in many instances, deviant behavior. There are very few minorities in Japan, with Koreans representing the largest group, but they number only approximately 600,000 in a total population of 115 million.

A second feature, which is not easily separated from the overall social fabric of Japanese life, is the large network of both formal and informal groups. Membership in a group or one's role in the group appears to be far more important than individuality, which is so highly prized in the United States. The emphasis on teamwork and the support Japanese offer one another clearly has implications for the low crime rate. Japanese family relationships are important in any discussion of the role of the group. Family members have a sense of responsibility for one another. The nature of this responsibility and the part played by family and larger community groups will be examined at length.

As a corollary to the closeness that develops through group life, the Japanese attempt to solve interpersonal conflict and seek harmony wherever possible. Japanese are fond of attributing their ability to get along with one another at least in part to the fact that they are living in a small island country. As I noted in an article for *The Japan Times*: "Japanese rarely act on feelings of hostility in public. A shove will not bring retaliation in a physical way, or probably even a verbal way. In Chicago, an obscene gesture could possibly result in your summary execution by the offended party. A shove in a New York subway might conceivably result in a knife between your ribs."[3]

The Japanese also help to discipline each other through informal assistance and intervention. While occasionally police have to assist drunks, fellow workers are far more likely to come to their assistance. In contrast, Americans tend not to associate in groups as often, and a drunk is more likely to have to rely on public officials for help than a colleague or friend. Group behavior helps the Japanese cope with the oppressiveness of modern urban life.

Related to these other social values is the powerful role of conformity. Despite the Westernization that has taken place in Japan since the Second World War, the pressure to conform is still very strong. The Japanese have a saying: "The nail that sticks up will get hammered down." American Fulbright lecturers, often unacquainted with Japanese society, express dismay that their students demonstrate little willingness to speak out and engage in energetic debate in class sessions. The Japanese student is afraid of standing out from the rest of his classmates. It is not unusual to hear of Japanese businessmen who have worked abroad for a number of years struggling to find their place in their companies upon returning to Japan. They may lose out on their promotions or advance at a different rate from their colleagues because they are suspected of having been tainted by their exposure to foreign ways. Similarly, students who receive their college education in the United States or other Western nations are sometimes handicapped when they have to compete with their Japanese-educated fellows for jobs. This sort of conformity, as will be seen, carries over into realms of crime and crime prevention.

The legal system reflects the value of conflict resolution through non-adversarial methods. There is considerably less litigation in Japan than in other industrialized nations. The first response to coping with a neighborhood problem is not to consult one's lawyer for advice, but to attempt to work out a compromise with one's potential adversary. Only three percent as many lawyers exist in Japan as in the United States—a figure that reflects this lesser demand for litigation.

The Japanese generally have much greater respect for legal and governmental institutions than do Americans, and the police benefit from this attitude. Unlike the situation in the United States, where police, particularly in larger cities, are beleaguered and viewed with suspicion, Japanese police are generally trusted and respected. The development of the legal system and the historical evolution of police services will be discussed in the next chapter.

In outlining some of the reasons for the low crime rate in Japan, one cannot ignore the strict gun control laws. In 1979, just 171 crimes were committed with guns. This is clearly one of the major reasons for the low rate of violent crime in Japan, and Americans could take a lesson from the Japanese in this respect. My Japanese colleagues indicated that they could not understand the obsession many Americans have with gun ownership.

Economic considerations are also important in accounting for Japan's comparatively low crime rate. Examining averages in Japan and the United States for income, production, and other economic factors is misleading because the figures often parallel each other in a general way, and do not disclose important underlying variations. Particularly important in the case of Japan is the generally high standard of living and the broad distribution of wealth among all social strata. Unemployment has remained low by American standards. Most Japanese consider themselves members of the middle class.

Skiing on some of Japan's winter slopes offers a glimpse of the affluence that is widespread. Rarely does one encounter a Japanese who is not dressed in a fashionable outfit. At the ski lodges of Hokkaido, waitresses on vacation are indistinguishable from wealthy matrons. In city areas where one might expect to find poverty and decay, such as near railway stations, one rarely comes upon the kind of derelict who is seen slumped over a bench in New York's Grand Central Station. Walking with police during their regular patrols in all types of neighborhoods in Tokyo and elsewhere, I rarely saw an entire section of a city bereft of resources, deteriorating, and run-down, as is so often the case in the inner cities in the United States.

Finally, in exploring the various reasons for Japan's low crime rate, a brief discussion of justice agencies and institutions—other than the police—will also be offered.

NOTES
1. H. Scott-Stokes, "In Japan, Crime Is Rare and Reaction Swift," *The New York Times*, April 12, 1981, p. E-7.
2. A. and H. Toffler, "Sifting Facts from Fiction about 1," *The Japan Times*, February 22, 1981, p. 8.
3. L. Craig Parker, "What the U.S. Can Do to Lessen Crime—Copy Japan," *The Japan Times*, January 18, 1981.

Chapter **2**

THE HISTORICAL AND LEGAL FRAMEWORK

Dispute Resolution

Japan has traditionally been described as a nation in which the formal system of justice, so eagerly embraced in the United States, is shunned, and extrajudicial informal procedures are sought. Historically, the whole concept of "dispute" has been an anathema to the Japanese, who prefer to see disagreements or conflicts between parties in a less aggressive light. As Kawashima suggests:

> Litigation presupposes and admits the existence of a dispute and leads to a decision which makes clear who is right or wrong in accordance with standards that are independent of the wills of the disputants. Furthermore, judicial decisions emphasize the conflict between the parties, deprive them of participation in the settlement, and assign a moral fault which can be avoided in a compromise solution.[1]

While Meiji government leaders near the end of the nineteenth century moved rapidly to introduce a European-style legal system in Japan, the deeply rooted feudalism of the Tokugawa period was not to be immediately overcome. Early innovations, such as the Penal Code of 1880 and the Criminal Procedure Code of 1890, reflected influence from the French system. Later, the Meiji legal system tended to show the Germanic (Prussian) influence that can be seen in many of the social and political reforms of the time. Tanabe comments on the reluctance of Japanese to engage in litigation in the wake of the implementation of these codes and statutes:

23

Under the long tradition of unusually strong governmental control and community pressure, the rights consciousness of the Japanese people was very low. Strong social and psychological pressures discouraged the filing of lawsuits, and manifold out-of-court resolution, techniques and mechanisms, such as mediation by relatives, court marshals, or local leaders, were commonly used. The compromise of civil disputes was generally regarded as the most desirable solution. In farming villages and small towns, suit against a neighbor was even a moral wrong.[2]

Even today, some contracts and agreements are still concluded orally without relying on lawyers. In other cases, a simple, written agreement might be drawn up by the parties themselves. Despite this historical reluctance to engage in litigation, change has been creeping in since the Second World War. Discussions with a wide variety of legal scholars, police officers, court personnel, and private citizens suggest that legal consciousness is growing in Japan. The number of cases brought to court has increased since the Second World War.

An interesting feature of the Japanese system of policing is that the availability of neighborhood police boxes allows citizens to seek out officers as informal arbiters of conflict. Citizens still rely on police for this type of counseling (known as *komarigoto sōdan*) and problem resolution to a far greater degree than do Americans. In general, the Japanese prefer a moral norm as opposed to a legal one for conflict resolution. Turning to a lawyer is admitting failure. According to Gibney:

> To the Japanese, the law is not a norm but a framework for discussion. The good Japanese judge is the man who can arrange and settle the most compromises out of court. When an American calls his lawyer, he is confident and happy to rely on the strength of his whole social system, the rule of law. When a Japanese calls his lawyer, he is sadly admitting that, in this case, his social system has broken down.[3]

Kawashima notes that there are two characteristics of the traditional social groups in Japan that have influenced the non-adversarial and extrajudicial approach to dispute resolution. First, there is the hierarchical feature where social status is clearly defined in terms of deference and authority. Family, community, and even contractual relationships are hierarchical. A contract of employment implies the deference of the employee to the employer; according to a contract of apprenticeship, the apprentice defers to the master; from a contract of sale, the seller defers to the buyer. Furthermore, Kawashima is quick to point out that the status of the master or employer is "patriarchal" and not "despotic." The implication is that the master or employer, while dominating in the relationship, will also give in and compromise on requests from the subordinate. This delicate balance of socially prescribed roles in Japan is alien to the American system of law and justice, which is based on fixed, universal standards.

A second characteristic of traditional social groups in Japan is that, between individuals of equal status, relationships have been both "particularistic" and "functionally diffuse." That is to say, for members of the same village community who are equal in social status, relationships are supposed to be "intimate" (a somewhat weakened version of the term as defined by Westerners), and their roles are defined vaguely and flexibly so that they lend themselves to adjustment whenever circumstances dictate. Thus, relationships are imbedded in a tradition that urges compromise, adjustment, and fluidity. Disputes are not supposed to arise, and the drawing up of formal, legal contracts only anticipates the breakdown of agreements between parties.

Private citizens are reluctant to invoke the law, but business firms are no more eager to engage in litigation.

> Japanese companies rarely sue each other, for example, over breach of contract; indeed, their written contracts usually aren't very specific in the first place. Executives from squabbling companies prefer to work their problems out through personal trust and understanding.[4]

Japanese businessmen do not arrive armed with lawyers at important conferences with government officials. There is a reluctance to sue because financial incentives are lacking. In anti-trust suits, for example, plaintiffs are not awarded "treble damages."

Kitagawa's discussion of field research on the lack of desire of Japanese to engage in litigation indicates similar findings: the motivation for the small number of proceedings is connected with the traditional social ordering structures. "From 65–75 percent of those questioned favored the extralegal methods of conciliation for resolution of legal disputes."[5] Large businesses in Japan have solved about 70–99 percent of their legal disputes through private reconciliation, while about 1–30 percent of such disputes have been brought to trial.

While the Japanese tradition has discouraged litigation, the United States has increasingly relied upon formal legal proceedings to resolve conflicts. Articles appear in American journals and magazines decrying the increase in the number of lawyers and litigation. In Auerbach's attack on the growth of law and the number of lawyers in the United States in "A Plague of Lawyers,"[6] he notes that the ratio of lawyers to the general population has grown from one lawyer for every 1,100 Americans at the beginning of the twentieth century to one for every 530 Americans in 1976. As McKay (1978) puts it, "Americans typically insist on more, not less, law as corrective."[7] He offers the efforts of Ralph Nader and his associates in the field of public interest law as one example of how social change has been accomplished through litigation in America. While I would disagree with the notion that Americans, given the choice, would opt for more law, it is clear that the open marketplace and the diversity of United States society have created an atmosphere in which law and litigation have grown without constraint. The lack of mediators or other forms of dispute resolution has spawned a massive legal profession and an unwieldy backlog in our courts.

The survey "Japanese Legal Consciousness," conducted by the Japan Culture Council (*Nihon Bunka Kaigi*), which sampled 1,500 people living in Tokyo in 1971, further documents the feelings of the Japanese about legal matters. Ames, in reporting on this survey, observed that both the formal (*tatemae*) and deeper gut-level feeling (*honne*) are revealed in the responses to three questions. Eighty-nine percent of the subjects stated that it is best to write up a contract no matter how much the two parties trust each other, and ninety percent felt that the contract should be very detailed in order to avoid misinterpretations—these attitudes might be termed *tatemae*. However, interestingly enough (and in apparent contradiction to the earlier responses), sixty-five percent felt that the contract could be abrogated by simply renegotiating with the other party when circumstances dictated; this view represents the *honne*, or underlying intention. While the first two responses are consistent with the Westernization of Japan, the latter one appears to stem from a more traditional Japanese view.

Another factor contributing to the apparent lack of litigation in Japan is that many matters normally reserved for licensed attorneys in the United States are handled by non-licensed lawyers in Japan. These non-licensed "lawyers" are usually graduates of law programs offered by Japanese colleges and universities at a level equivalent to undergraduate education in the United States. If one wishes to become a practicing lawyer, judge, or public prosecutor, one must apply for admission to the two-year course at the Judicial and Legal Training Institute. Admission standards at this institute are extremely high. Competition is so severe that even a graduate of Tokyo University's elite law faculty is far from being assured a place in the typical class of 500, chosen from over 30,000 yearly applicants.

Japanese universities, like the rest of the society, are hierarchically ranked, with Tokyo University coming first in most fields, and the prestige of graduating from such an institution assures a variety of options, even for those not admitted to the Judicial and Legal Training Institute. For example, a majority of the members of the elite class of bureaucrats at the National Police Agency are Tokyo University law faculty graduates. Only ten to twenty of those who successfully pass the National Public Service Examination each year are admitted to this special class, hereafter referred to as the "elite" program, as assistant inspectors. The majority of these young officers eventually become chiefs of the forty-seven prefectural police agencies or assume other top posts. In general, national governmental positions that carry responsibility are considered prestigious choices in Japan and are open primarily to graduates of the upper-ranked universities.

Of the dozen or more high-ranking officers I interviewed or worked with at the headquarters of the National Police Agency in Tokyo, all were graduates of the law faculty at Tokyo University. While these graduates frequently seek employment in the various national ministries and bureaucracies, they also find their way into positions of prominence in business and elsewhere, and thus their work may not be legal in nature, despite their having completed an undergraduate degree in law.

Studying law at a university in Japan is similar to most undergraduate majors in the United States; the first one and a half years are quite general, while the last two and a half years are more specialized. Graduates of these programs, while not designated as lawyers, are able to draft wills, litigate small claims, offer tax advice, and write contracts. Most of these same functions are performed in the United States by lawyers who have passed state bar examinations. Japan now has approximately 12,000 lawyers serving a population of 115 million, compared to the 600,000 lawyers practicing in the United States, with a population just a little more than twice Japan's.

The Japanese concept of rights also has a bearing on the attitude toward litigation. The expectation that agreements will be kept and obligations met makes the notion of "demanding one's rights" something of an anomaly. Historically, the individual's rights have been subservient to the needs of the group in Japan. Kawashima explains that the individual's desires are "absorbed in the interest of the collectivity to which he belongs, and the interest of the collectivity is recognized as having primary importance, while the interest of the individual has merely a secondary importance."[8] Walter Ames, in his study of police in Japan, notes that the previously mentioned survey of legal consciousness suggests a greater awareness of rights now than before the Occupation. He continues:

> In a question about the priority of individual rights or the

priority of the public welfare, the answers were almost equally divided (forty-eight percent felt the public welfare should take precedence over individual rights, while forty-two percent felt the opposite).[9]

During interviews with police officers who were working out of the mini-police stations in various cities, I frequently asked the question, "What has changed the most during your career?" Numerous responses were received on the theme of "citizens' awareness of their rights." Not surprisingly, the police viewed this growth in the number of people citing their rights as making their job more difficult. Younger citizens, in particular, are less compliant than they used to be. Human rights commissions have flourished all over Japan since the end of the Second World War, and a "Human Rights Protection Commission" exists in every prefecture.

The erosion of traditional values, which provided a braking effect on the growth of criminal behavior, and the increased reliance on law were evident to Hirano more than fifteen years ago:

> The role of criminal law as an agency of social control will become more pervasive, since nonlegal forms of control such as the family and community will surely become less and less powerful. At the same time, criminal law will become more functional and less moralistic.[10]

Historical Trends

While a detailed history of Japan's judicial system is beyond the scope of this work, some observations concerning the beginnings of the police system seem appropriate. During the feudal period of the Tokugawa Shogunate, from 1603 to 1867, there were four clearly defined classes. At the top were the samurai, who were the warriors and the military arm of the feudal lords, or *daimyō*. They were followed by the peasants, the artisans, and the merchants. The class system of this time was very strict and upward movement was difficult—you were born into a class and you stayed there throughout your lifetime. Loyalty to the government and to one's family characterized this period, and there was little reliance on formal law. Hirano notes that throughout Japanese history:

> It is not the awareness of punishment which serves to deter a Japanese so much as the awareness of the impact which the fact of his involvement in criminal proceedings would have on himself and, more important, on his family.[11]

Westney (1982) notes that formalized police services as we know them today did not appear until the Meiji period. Instead, samurai attached to government agencies acted as police. Their activities were overseen by magistrates assigned to cities and towns. Samurai alone were entitled to wear weapons during this period, and wore two swords in their belts, one three or four feet long and the other two, which served both as weapons and as symbols of rank. Attached to his status was not only the power but the obligation to act as a kind of policeman. At least officially they had the right to draw their sword and kill a commoner who deviated in any way from the proper social role. Samurai, particularly lower-ranking samurai, were sensitive about this status prerogative and tended to draw their swords at the slightest provocation. Examples of behavior that deviated from the norm included not bowing low enough or not kneeling when the feudal lord's procession was passing. A number of international incidents occurred during the 1850s and 1860s in which samurai retainers cut down Westerners who did not kneel when the procession of a feudal lord was passing.

Japanese society during this period resembled fifteenth-century Europe in some respects. The country was divided into some 245 feudal domains, the *shōgun*, or overlord, being in overall control. The well-ordered system of social relationships was based on Confucian principles that had been imported from China. In some respects Japan is still a Confucian society, the vertical and hierarchical structure being perhaps its most salient feature. But society of the Tokugawa period was even more hierarchical, with an elaborate system of social obligations that were used as an indirect, but nonetheless powerful, means of suppression.

To the Meiji emperor and his government fell the difficult task of rapidly modernizing a nation that had been in seclusion for centuries. The apparatus of the feudal empire was dismantled within a few years after the Meiji Restoration, and a program of modernization, that is, Westernization, was begun by the new government. Many scholars, both Western and Japanese, have noted that the changes were in no small measure brought about to improve upon the treaties that had been foisted upon the Japanese by Western governments. A particular irritant was the fact that Westerners had refused to permit their own people to be prosecuted under native law for criminal offenses but insisted instead on administering their own justice. To alleviate this situation and provide Japan with a legal system acceptable to Westerners, as noted earlier, codes of criminal law were adopted, first on the French model and later on the German.

The concept of human rights in Japan cannot be fully understood without exploring the relationship of the emperor to his subjects. One description of the role of the emperor dating from the early Meiji period states that:

> [He] possessed both political power and spiritual authority, [and] embodied the perquisites of both the German emperor and the Pope. The people were not only the emperor's subjects politically but his followers spiritually. In addition to enacting laws, the emperor issued imperial rescripts on education, national esprit and morality. The people were required to observe the law in their overt behavior and were also obliged to order their consciences in accord with imperial rescripts. A portrait of the emperor was enshrined in every school, and the principal often read rescripts aloud. Moreover, all subjects were required to stand in awed attention when facing the emperor's portrait or when listening to rescripts. Insofar as the arbiter of spiritual values and political authority were one, ethics and power, public and private [*ōyake* and *watakushi*], were completely fused together.[12]

A different perspective of the role of the individual in the Meiji state is offered in the government's "The Way of the Subject" (*Shimin no michi*):

What we call our private life amounts, in the final analysis, to the practice of the Way of the Subject, and takes on public significance as we carry out our duty to assist in imperial rule. . . . Thus even while engaged in private activities, we must never forget our duty to devote ourselves to the emperor and serve the state. In our country everything one does—whether he is in government or in private business, whether he is a parent raising children or a son studying in school—is in fulfillment of his particular duty as an imperial subject.[13]

The obligations to the state are abundantly clear. Basing their power on this kind of obedience, the Meiji leaders established an authoritarian regime that was intolerant of opposition to its policies. Early champions of civil rights movements were put down by direct police intervention or through more devious methods.

Most social scientists agree that the authoritarian spirit, like its philosophical version, Confucianism, survives to some extent in modern Japan. Ishida (1968) notes that while protest activity in Japan has become more common, nonetheless "the tradition of saying no is very weak among Japanese." Ike (1972) refers to a "preference for paternalism," and Koschmann, commenting on Japan's history, says of the Japanese that "Never conquered by or directly confronted with external forms of political rule, they remained unaware of the potentially relative, fallible nature of all authority. Authority was a 'given,' taken for granted as an unalienable part of the natural order."[14]

Matsumoto, professor of Japanese political thought at Tokyo University, has observed that:

There is an assumption that the state is a prior and self-justifying entity, sufficient in itself. This results in the belief that political functions, and the existence, maintenance and development of the state should take precedence over the goals of other individuals and associations, or at least, that the former are more important than the latter.[15]

The structural outline and character of Japan's present-day police force were already visible in the Meiji era. Features inherited from that period include the "routine family visits" to households by police officers, and the scattering of police boxes—*kōban* and *chū-zaisho*—throughout the country. (*Kōban* are police boxes or mini-stations in cities, while *chūzaisho* are rural police boxes that are residential in character, typically with a staff of one officer and accommodation for the officer's family in the rear of the building.)

During the early days of the Meiji era, the nation was in a state of turbulence and the new government found it difficult to maintain order. Uprisings and bloodshed occurred in many places; people felt apprehensive and fearful. According to Kanetake-Oura:

> There was not lacking a rough element which, dissatisfied with the new Government, watched for an opportunity to rise against it. Moreover, many ruffians at large constituted a danger to the people. The main object of the police at that time was to arrest these malcontents and bravadoes.[16]

Clearly, this task required a strong police force.

The structure of the force that was established was highly centralized and powerful, and police duties embraced a variety of activities that would be foreign to most modern forces. For example, public health, sanitation, construction, and fire-fighting activities were all under police jurisdiction. Despite having control of these public services, police in the Meiji period, unlike today, were not considered public servants. Instead, their principle functions were surveillance and political control. As a police bureau chief of the time put it: "There would be no household in Japan into which the eyes of the police would not see and the ears would not hear."[17]

This task of surveillance and control was carried out by a force of three thousand former samurai, a fact which soon proved to be a problem in itself. Individuals who were used to functioning on the basis of their social status had to be taught to function within an organizational structure. Sugai comments on the pluses and minuses of a police force made up of former samurai:

> This method of choosing men was singularly effective in guaranteeing their staunchness and relative immunity from

corruption because of a system of morality peculiar to the former warrior class. On the other hand, this practice had certain drawbacks in that it tended to develop in the police an attitude of disrespect and superciliousness toward the people.

Anticipating the potential problems, the Meiji government hit upon one idea to facilitate control of the police force: two-thirds of the men selected came from just one province in Kyushu. This practice of selecting police for the Tokyo Metropolitan Police Department from other regions of Japan is still prevalent. It is believed that police officers working in areas away from their place of birth avoid the problems of enforcing the law with relatives and friends.

Westney explains that the police department was patterned after a combination of the Paris Prefecture of Police and the Yokohama Police Department. While it was the Tokyo Police Department that eventually emerged as the model for other Japanese police departments, it was Yokohama—partly because of the large number of foreigners who lived there—that actually had the first department in Japan. Westerners residing in Yokohama were familiar with effective policing and pressed for its development. Prior to 1868, the foreign community itself was responsible for policing, and because Englishmen were predominant, the Yokohama police reflected "the English model of organization, drill, patrolling system, and weaponry."[18]

While the Tokyo police initially retained the flavor of the English-style Yokohama force, with the transfer of the police operation from the Tokyo Prefectural Government to the Ministry of Justice, the organization was revised. A group of officials was sent abroad to study police departments in a number of countries— France, Belgium, Germany, Russia, Austria, and Italy. The French approach, however, was apparently favored from the outset, and it was French influence that eventually shaped the Tokyo Police Department. The French model, under which the police had wide-ranging administrative functions and a high degree of political involvement, was particularly appealing to the Japanese. The police department that was created in Tokyo controlled other services, such as fire-fighting, prisons, and health, and became a "powerful and virtually autonomous organization that like its model played a central role in the life of the national capital and had close ties to the central government."[19]

The biannual "routine family visits" that police conduct today in Japan had their origin at this time. Again, Westney's account is most useful. She explains that during the Meiji period, police gathered information that included the name, occupation, age, and social status of each resident. While today all households are supposed to be visited twice annually, during this earlier period the frequency was contingent upon one's social status. Property owners and people of high reputation were visited just once a year. People of lesser status—including those who did not own property— were visited twice annually. Finally, those who were unemployed or had criminal records were subjected to three visits annually.

The police function was moved in 1874 from the Ministry of Justice to the Ministry of Home Affairs. The new police agency was named the Police Bureau and it continued under the Home Ministry until it was abolished in 1947. The Metropolitan Police Department was established in Tokyo, and prefectural governors were given jurisdiction over their respective police forces.

> Salaries, travel allowances, etc. of police officers above inspector's rank were paid from the national treasury; other expenses, such as maintaining policemen in lower ranks and providing and keeping up office buildings, were mainly met by local taxes but partially subsidized by the national government—the ratio of subsidies being four-tenths of all expenses for the Metropolitan Police Board and one-sixth for other prefectures.[20]

The cooperation in the Meiji period between the national and prefectural governments for the support of police services is roughly similar to the organizational breakdown that presently exists between the National Police Agency and prefectural police agencies (for example, currently the National Police Agency pays the salaries of all officers at the rank of Senior Superintendent or above).

As noted above, the system of *kōban* and *chūzaisho* also had its inception during the Meiji period, and there were more than four hundred police boxes throughout the city of Tokyo in 1877. In addition to the buildings themselves, the method of staffing them has also been preserved, especially in the high ratio of supervisors to patrolmen. During the Meiji period, one officer supervised three patrolmen at a *kōban*; one walked the beat, one was stationed outside, and one was on duty inside processing paperwork. The pattern is strikingly similar today.

Kōban were placed at transportation centers, major intersections, shopping areas, at entrances to public parks, near the entrances to temple areas, and at other locations where people congregated and where crime might be expected to occur. The term *kōban* had originally been used to identify the dormitory-like buildings in Tokyo in which police lived, but was later applied to non-residential urban police boxes. Police boxes have officially been called *hashutsujo* since 1888, but the term *kōban* persists.

One of the early legal statements on the role of police during the Meiji era was described by Kanetake-Oura in 1910:

> 1. Fundamental Laws Relating to the Police System
> (a) The Constitution of the Empire of Japan—1889. Art. 9. The Emperor issues, or causes to be issued, the ordinances necessary for the carrying out of the laws, or for the maintenance of the public peace and order, and for the promotion of the welfare of the subjects.
> (b) Regulations relating to the Administrative Police (drawn up in 1875).

These regulations defined for the first time in Japan the sphere and aim of police authority, and indicated the functions of police administration. We mention here some important articles of these regulations:

> Art. 1. The object of the administrative police is to anticipate evils threatening the people and so to preserve the latter's safety.
> Art. 2. The local governor (except in the prefecture of Tokyo)

superintends the police affairs of the locality, appoints police sergeants to their respective duties, and dispatches them, whenever necessary, to different places, to overlook policemen in the discharge of their duties.

The business of the police is divided into the following four parts:

(1) Protecting the people from wrong-doers.
(2) Acting as sanitary inspectors.
(3) Checking lewdness and profligacy.
(4) Detecting and providing against persons who contemplate acts contrary to the established laws of the land.

Art. 5. The police shall aim at preserving public welfare, and in no case shall one pry into petty incidents of family affairs, nor use his position to gain profit for himself.[21]

Neighborhood Associations

Associations in which neighbors assisted each other in a variety of activities, such as planting rice, building houses, and other aspects of daily living, were an integral part of the social fabric during the Meiji era. The general term for these groups is *tonari-gumi*. In rural areas they were called *burakukai* and in urban areas *chōnaikai*. Approximately, ten to twenty families formed one *tonari-gumi*.

The neighborhood associations are important in considering crime control because they were the forerunners of crime prevention associations. *Tonari-gumi* existed up to the time of the Occupation, when they were forced to disband by the Allied forces. They have since re-formed, though their influence is much weaker. Western authorities suspected them of being part of the prewar authoritarian apparatus, with leaders using coercive and autocratic tactics in dealings with group members, since the leaders of these groups were reputed to have been extremely loyal to the emperor and the government, and it was not uncommon for both members and leaders to report secretly on citizens who departed from government policy. In the early period of their existence, the heads of the neighborhood associations were appointed by the city government chiefs, while later they were elected.

In the prewar period, these government-appointed heads of the neighborhood associations had close working relationships with the police officials in their area. The *burakukai* and *chōnaikai* maintained their own meeting halls, and these served as centers of community activity. The *tonari-gumi* were semi-official arms of the police and were used in the general task of keeping order.

In postwar Japan, the status of these groups and their relations with the police are somewhat different. In place of the disbanded neighborhood associations, local crime prevention groups have formed with a narrower framework. To some extent the ties with the police remain close, but the leadership is now elected, and some friction with the authorities has been known to occur, especially around election time, when it is not uncommon to have *chōnaikai* members arrested for campaign violations.

Today, the *burakukai* and *chōnaikai* continue to function in outlying areas, but Japanese authorities claim that their strength has dwindled in the cities due to the unwillingness of unmarried residents of apartments and condominiums to join. Conversely, residents of very small apartments are sometimes excluded from *chōnaikai* because they are perceived to be short-term residents of the area. The perception is not unjustified, since occupants of these units move, on the average, once every two years.

Historically, the neighborhood *tonari-gumi* were involved in a variety of social and civic activities. For example, on the occasion of a birth or wedding, a sum of money was collected by the head of the group, who likewise organized assistance for the families of deceased persons. A variety of obligations and rituals was involved with participation in such neighborhood groups, and individuals who were able to engage in these forms of social intercourse with skill and confidence felt a sense of accomplishment and self-esteem. The network of social and neighborhood obligations involves the complex notion of *giri*, literally "duty," which is considered a basic principle of social interaction in Japan, though most scholars agree that its influence has decreased in recent years. While the traditional *tonari-gumi* were broken up by the Occupation forces, many of their functions were adopted by newly formed neighborhood groups.

It is not difficult to imagine the ways in which the network of relationships that became established through the *tonari-gumi* and their modern counterparts lent itself to crime prevention activity. Among the wide variety of neighborhood obligations, crime prevention was just one more aspect of community life. The modern-day crime prevention associations will be discussed at greater length in a later chapter.

The Suppression of Radicals

The strong repressive measures taken by the government against radical leftists during the pre–Second World War period have been described by Mitchell (1976), Okudaira (1973), and others. Their descriptions of the atmosphere surrounding the promulgation of the Peace Preservation Law and related laws, along with the sweeping enforcement of it by police and prosecutors, paint an ugly picture. The general turbulence of the times, combined with the rise of left-wing radicals, resulted in the passing of the Peace Preservation Law in 1925. The office of the Police Bureau in the Home Ministry was particularly active at this time. Okudaira, in particular, captures the mood of the period:

> The dangerous thoughts, which the Peace Preservation Law raised as the subject of control, implied, in the beginning, Communism and anarchism, and later the implication of the term "dangerous" became more and more stretched, and finally every anti-government thought—the identifications were made by the administration of each period—was regarded to be under the application of the law. The victims of the Peace Preservation Law were not only those who attempted to reform the then-existing Buddhism, the believers in Shintoism or in the numerous newly risen religions but also those belonging to "Jehovah's Witnesses," "Seventh-day Adventists," and the "No-church Independent Sect." On the other hand, the controlling authorities attached great importance to cultural movements along with labor and political movements. Con-

sequently, students' researches in the social sciences or the liberal arts were the most important subjects of restraint.[22]

An earlier law that was also repressive in nature was the Public Police Law of 1900. This law was aimed at antigovernment political groups, but it also restricted organized labor. These political groups were required to register their programs with the police, and they needed permission to meet. Their meetings could be dissolved by the police and their organizations disbanded, and membership in secret organizations was prohibited. Violators could be punished by fines and up to one year in prison.

It was left primarily to the Home Ministry's Police Bureau to suppress radicals and control protest movements, and unlike the situation in Western countries, where political organizations and publications were regulated through the courts, in Japan police used administrative techniques to maintain public order. Faced with increasing left-wing radicalism, in 1902 the government created a Higher Police Unit and a second unit, the Special Higher Police. The repressive machinery of the Japanese justice system of the prewar period appears to have emerged for a variety of reasons in addition to those already mentioned. Mitchell explains:

> The reasons for thought control in Japan were complex and not confined to flaws in the Meiji Constitution, a tradition of authoritarianism, and the weakness of liberalism. Other factors less subject to direct manipulation by Japan's leaders must be considered: the rapidity with which the whole world's economic system collapsed and the more uncompromising attitudes of China and the United States. These problems, together with the rise of Communism, signified the weakening of the old economic and political order.[23]

Mitchell explains that prosecutors were powerful during the 1920s. They dressed like judges, identifying themselves closely with the judiciary. They helped in the drafting of court documents and handling of cases, and frequently played the role of preliminary judges. One of the tools of the prosecutors' wide-ranging power was the designation "charges withheld." The individual was neither prosecuted nor totally absolved of charges. He was cast into a probationary limbo, under the jurisdiction of the prosecutor. Any further violations were sure to result in vigorous prosecution.

The control and suppression that characterized the political climate of the early Meiji period is reflected in Okudaira's comment on the role of censorship in enforcing government policy. The control of newspapers shifted from "prepublication" censorship to a less direct "postpublication" censorship, in which heavy penalties were extracted from writers and editors who affronted the government censors. Legislation enacted in 1875 placed the "seat of censorship" within the Police Bureau of the Home Ministry, and books regarded as detrimental to the public peace could be seized and the presses that printed them destroyed. Publications were scrutinized by justice officials, and the head of the Book Section of the Special Higher Police stated: "We prohibited things which were against public order and good morals."[24]

Both those who worked against the intent of the law and those who were obedient were subject to that arrogance with which public officials generally treated average citizens, and it is not surprising that some older Japanese still have a bitter, resentful feeling toward the police. This anger, mixed with anxiety, occasionally emerged in my interviews with older citizens.

Policing after the Second World War

During the period after the Second World War, police jurisdiction became more limited in scope, though it is still broader than in the United States. The Occupation forces imposed a decentralized system of police agencies in 1947, and all cities and towns with more than five thousand residents were required to maintain their own police departments. The responsibilities of the police were limited to "maintaining peace and order in Japan, investigating crimes, and protecting the life and property of the nation."[25] To assume some of the functions removed from police work, the Public Safety Commission system was introduced at both national and prefectural levels. Fire protection, health services, and other non-police functions were assigned to other agencies. The police were to concentrate on "standards, identification, communication, training, scientific crime detection and statistics."[26]

The National Police Agency's publication *The Police of Japan* politely refers to the deep dismay of Japanese government authorities at the decentralization of police by describing "organizational defects" and "heavy financial burdens." Those "inefficiencies" were corrected when the Police Law of 1954 was adopted and the national character of the police services was restored. The Public Safety Commissions were retained, and all municipal and rural police agencies were integrated under the framework of the forty-seven prefectural police departments.

An historical view of Japanese justice is necessary to understand today's system of policing. A number of specific features such as the "routine family visits" of the Meiji era have been carried over virtually intact. The attitudes of present-day citizens toward the police have been shaped, in part, by the police behavior of the Meiji and pre–Second World War periods. Legal concepts rooted in Confucian doctrine continue to affect dispute resolution in Japan, and the attempt at democratization of the Japanese justice apparatus has resulted in, among other things, a greater concern for human rights.

NOTES
1. T. Kawashima, "Dispute Resolution in Contemporary Japan." In A. Von Mehren, ed., *Law in Japan: The Legal Order in a Changing Society* (Cambridge, Massachusetts: Harvard University Press, 1963), p. 43.
2. K. Tanabe, "The Processes of Litigation: An Experiment with the Adversary System." *Ibid.*, p. 77.
3. Frank Gibney, *Japan: The Fragile Superpower* (New York: W. W. Norton, 1975), p. 82.
4. A. Meyerson, "Legal Profession in Japan: A Small Guild," *The Asian Wall Street Journal*, February 17, 1981, p. 4.
5. Z. Kitagawa, "Method of Solving Legal Disputes in Japan." In *Materials on Legal Institutions in Japan*, 1–49, Multilith, 1974, p. 78.
6. J. Auerbach, "A Plague of Lawyers," *Harper's Magazine*, 253, October 1976.
7. R. McKay, "Japan: Streets without Crimes, Disputes without Lawyers." Unpublished manuscript, Aspen Institute Program on Justice, Society and the Individual, 1978.
8. T. Kawashima, "The Status of the Individual and the Notion of Law, Right, and Social Order in Japan." In Charles A. Moore, ed., *The Japanese Mind: Essentials of Japanese Philosophy and Culture* (Honolulu: East-West Center Press, 1967), p. 264.

9. Walter L. Ames, "Police and Community in Japan." Unpublished thesis, Ann Arbor, Michigan: University of Michigan, 1976, p. 239.

10. R. Hirano, "The Accused and Society: Some Aspects of Japanese Criminal Law." In A. Von Mehren, ed., *op. cit.*, p. 295.

11. *Ibid.*, p. 291.

12. O. Kuno, "The Meiji State, Minponshugi, and Ultranationalism." In J. Victor Koschmann, ed., *Authority and the Individual in Japan* (Tokyo: University of Tokyo Press, 1978), p. 61.

13. *Ibid.*, p. 62.

14. J. Victor Koschmann, "Soft Rule and Expressive Protest." In J. Victor Koschmann, ed., *op. cit.*, p. 7.

15. S. Matsumoto, "The Roots of Political Disillusionmnent: 'Public and Private' in Japan." In J. Victor. Koschmann, ed., *op. cit.*, p. 38.

16. B. Kanetake-Oura, *Fifty Years of New Japan* (London: Smith Elder & Co., 1910), p. 283.

17. S. Sugai, "The Japanese Police System." In R. Ward, ed., *Five Studies in Japanese Politics* (Ann Arbor, Michigan: University of Michigan Press, Center for Japanese Studies, Occasional Papers, No. 7, 1957), p. 4.

18. E. Westney, "The Emulation of Western Organizations in Meiji Japan: The Case of Paris Prefecture of Police and the Keishi-Cho," *The Journal of Japanese Studies*, 8, No. 2, 1982, p. 4.

19. *Ibid.*, p. 11.

20. Sugai, *op. cit.*, p. 4.

21. Kanetake-Oura, *op. cit.*, p. 287.

22. Y. Okudaira, "Some Preparatory Notes for the Study of the Peace and Preservation Law in Prewar Japan," *Annals of the Institute of Social Science* (University of Tokyo Press, 1973), p. 49.

23. Richard H. Mitchell, *Thought Control in Prewar Japan* (Ithaca, New York: Cornell University Press, 1976), p. 192.

24. *Ibid.*, p. 29.

25. National Police Agency of Japan, *The Police of Japan*, 1980, p. 5.

26. Ames, *op. cit.*, p. 239.

Chapter 3

KŌBAN POLICE

The Tokyo Metropolitan Police Department

This study of police behavior is based upon visits, interviews, and observations of police at work in a variety of locations, including Tokyo, Chiba, Kobe, Sapporo, Yokohama, and Kyoto, as well as some rural areas. Initially, I concentrated on the Tokyo Metropolitan Police Department (M.P.D.).

A glossy piece of public relations literature published by the Tokyo Metropolitan Police Department proudly notes:

> Tokyo is the center of government, business, culture and transportation of Japan, with a population of over 11,681,000 in an area of 2,145 square kilometers (828 square miles). The total personnel of the M.P.D., which has been increasing annually, was 44,238, which included 3,162 civilians and 1,300 policewomen for the period ending in December, 1979. There were approximately 15,000 police assigned to the patrol section.[1]

While the plans for my study were coordinated with officials of the National Police Agency, a direct, personal introduction by a Tokyo Public Safety Commission member to a police administrator at the Tokyo Metropolitan Police Department provided the key to studying police in Tokyo. As noted previously, personal introductions are of critical importance in paving the way for any project in Japan. The series of planning sessions that ensued required visits to the Tokyo Metropolitan Police Department's

44

new headquarters and offered a glimpse of police activities that are in marked contrast with the service-oriented work of the patrol officer on the beat. (The Japanese refer to the patrol officer as *omawari-san*, meaning something close to "Mr. Walk-around.")

The new headquarters looms like a fortress near the Imperial Palace grounds. The atmosphere inside is very formal and a bit startling if one is unprepared for the military demeanor of the police personnel on duty. Officers guard the entrance and uniformed women await visitors behind a desk inside. Arriving officials are greeted with the equivalent of a snap to attention and are crisply saluted. Impeccably dressed officers issue identifying badges to visitors, who are required to wait for an escort before proceeding to a particular conference area or office in the eighteen-story building.

The administrative head of the Patrol Division and three of his assistants were assigned to assist in my research. In addition to the patrol head's three assistants, the planning sessions included my interpreter and the M.P.D.'s interpreter. One officer kept careful notes of all discussions—he even made a written note of the fact that my interpreter had graduated from Keio University. Plans were worked out for the ensuing three months over cups of green tea. Generally the atmosphere was cordial and friendly and we even managed to share a bit of humor. I was eager to allay any anxiety on their part about my intentions by clearly defining the scope of the study. I made requests to visit police boxes, to interview police officers, to observe officer–citizen contact, and to observe certain programs (for example, the counseling centers for juvenile offenders and pre-delinquent youth). In addition, I wanted flexibility to pursue other interests that might develop during my research. I realized that in all of this it was important to have the support of these administrators.

One of my main objectives was to learn about police–community relations. I decided to begin at the grass roots level, that is, with the daily work of police at *kōban* and *chūzaisho*, and requested permission to spend time in a variety of locations within the Tokyo Metropolitan Police Department's jurisdiction—areas that would reflect different socioeconomic conditions and offer

The new headquarters of the Tokyo Metropolitan Police Department, opened in 1980.

a wide exposure to Japanese urban life. With this in mind, the following stations were mutually agreed upon: Tsukiji/Ginza (an entertainment and shopping center); Shitaya (an older commercial and working-class residential section); Seijō (a quiet, upper-class residential section some distance from downtown); Akabane (a somewhat commercial, lower-middle-class area in the north, which includes large housing projects); and Motofuji (a region that encompasses a campus of Tokyo University).

In order to understand the *kōban* system, it is useful to see it (and most other Japanese police activities) as an outgrowth of the well-known Japanese penchant for order. The most salient feature of this orderly system is a national standardization that would be both foreign and enviable to an American policeman accustomed to the varied behavior of the thousands of different police agencies in the United States. In America, with most towns, municipalities, and states operating their own autonomous police departments, the differences in patterns and styles of policing are taken for granted. For example, some departments are "service-oriented," while others may emphasize "keeping order." In Japan the police force is organized nationally, and a number of benefits result.

One of the most notable of these is the high level of professionalism among police officers. A professional is one who emphasizes public service, has high standards of performance, a broad knowledge of his or her field, and participates in professional conferences and associations. When measured by the standards set by law and medicine, police in both Japan and the United States fall short of the mark, primarily because independence of judgment and action is lost in the demands of the organization. Japanese police, however, with the advantage of being unfettered by the demands of labor unions, come closer to meeting the classic sociological criteria for professionalism.

Westney, in her discussion of the history of the Japanese police during the Meiji period, suggests that encouraging professionalism was

> a means of reducing turnover in the force and of improving police standards of performance without a marked increase in expenditures, and it facilitated the standardization of police practice throughout the country. However, it had other, unanticipated consequences: it increased the autonomy of the police force, it reduced its responsiveness to its social environment, and it reinforced the social distance between the policeman and the public.[2]

The foundation for contemporary policing was set during this period, and the continuity of certain features is remarkable. An extremely important question raised by Westney has to do with the price of police professionalism in Japan: are police less responsive to the social environment and has the social distance between the police and the public been reinforced? Whether the benefits outweigh the disadvantages is open to question, but it is certain that dedication and commitment to the job run high among Japanese police. An American legal affairs officer assigned to the U.S. Embassy in Tokyo, who has worked with the police over a number of years remarked, "They're not wondering if they can step out of police work and find a better-paying job like American police."

Entrance standards and training are rigorously controlled by the National Police Agency. Undoubtedly major economic savings are obtained as a result of this coordinated national system. In recent years, the Tokyo Metropolitan Police Department has been able to attract an increasing number of college graduates. Officials informed me that in 1975, forty percent of those selected were college graduates, while sixty percent had completed high school. By 1980, those percentages were reversed. Nationally, approximately fifty percent of the police recruits are graduates of four-year colleges and universities.

Though the United States cannot claim such figures for entering personnel, the American system is clearly ahead of the Japanese in offering college-level courses for officers once they have joined. As of 1980–81, Japan had no academic degree programs intended for working justice personnel. Thus, while a larger percentage of entering police personnel possess college degrees in Japan, there are fewer opportunities for the average police officer to obtain a degree once he or she is on the job. Criminology programs or criminal justice programs are not available, nor apparently is there much demand for them.

College-level degree programs for police in America started increasing only after the riots of the sixties. The Law Enforcement Assistance Administration of the Justice Department provided grants so that public justice employees could pursue degrees.

However, the quality of education varied greatly, and some colleges offered very inferior education for police and other justice personnel.

The recruiting examination for Japanese police candidates includes a written examination on general educational subjects, a composition, an aptitude test, a physical examination, and, finally, a thorough assessment of each applicant's character evaluated by means of a personal interview.

Training periods for American police vary from several weeks to six months or more. In Japan, candidates who are high school graduates must complete one full year of training, while college graduates are trained for six months. Additional on-the-job training at police stations is offered by selected sergeants. This is followed by an in-service supplementary course of four months.

Officers are also required to become proficient in kendo (Japanese swordsmanship) and judo, and they continue to maintain their physical condition by pursuing these sports after they complete the training academy program. Older police have "seasonal" (winter and summer) practice on a once-a-week basis.

The basic starting salary for a high school graduate who has completed the required one-year course is ¥1,146,000, or $4,982 (exchange rate of ¥230 per dollar), for the year 1979 (National Police Agency, 1980). Since annual bonuses awarded to all police are the equivalent of approximately five months' salary, this represents an additional ¥481,320, or $2,092. While this total salary is only $7,074, there are a variety of other benefits for the young officer. "Family allowances" and "community allowances" are quite liberal, and they cover dependents, housing, commuting, assignment to supervisory positions, overtime, and working nights and holidays. With extremely inexpensive housing—dormitory-style for single personnel—made available, along with a broad medical plan, the new police officer's financial status compares quite favorably with entry-level workers in other fields. For instance, the National Police Agency is quick to point out that ordinary public service personnel start at a base pay of only ¥81,400 per month—¥14,000 less than a police officer.

The average annual entrance salary for full-time police officers in the United States was $12,152 in 1979 for cities over 10,000 in population. For larger American cities, the figures were somewhat higher: New York City, $14,220; San Francisco, $16,389; Washington, D.C., $14,558; Los Angeles, $15,931 (International City Management Association, 1980). However, comparisons are extremely difficult due to the benefit system in Japan and discrepancies in the cost of living both between the two countries and within the countries themselves.

The working hours of officers within the M.P.D. are quite unlike the shift patterns of American police. Typically, American police work rotating shifts. For example, they might work several weeks on the "graveyard" shift (night work: 11 P.M. to 7 A.M.), followed by either several weeks of a 7 A.M. to 3 P.M. shift or a 3 P.M. to 11 P.M. shift. In some departments, newly recruited officers will be on the "graveyard" shift for an extended period due to their lack of seniority. Because of the large number of departments it is impossible to generalize about nationwide patterns in the United States. The aforementioned schedules are just examples from departments I have become familiar with in the eastern section of the country.

The pattern in Japan is very different. Police stationed at *kōban* and assigned to patrol work in the Tokyo M.P.D. work the following schedule (there do appear to be slight variations in some cases):

1st day: 9:00 A.M. to 5:15 P.M.
2nd day: 8:30 A.M. to 5:15 P.M.
3rd day: 2:00 P.M. to 9:30 A.M. (Frequently officers do not actually get off duty until 10:00 A.M. or 11:00 A.M. on this last day. They claim that they sleep only about four hours, but officially they are entitled to more rest.)
4th day: Off

The hours for detectives and other personnel assigned to specialized duties vary from this, but approximately forty-four to forty-eight hours per week are standard for M.P.D. personnel. Overtime is common, and this adds to the total hours accumulated.

Kōban usually have several small rooms. The glass-enclosed room in front has a desk. The rear rooms, or occasionally an upstairs room, provide a *tatami* mat area for sleeping and sometimes a separate room for preparing modest meals. (*Tatami* mats are approximately three feet by six feet and consist of a thick base of straw, covered with woven rushes.) A concealed safe is available for locking up weapons while the officer is asleep. *Kōban* vary tremendously in size and shape, but they tend to be crowded, a condition typical of Japanese housing as well.

Though the police have few complaints, the dilapidated condition of some *kōban* is the frequent cause of some grumbles. An M.P.D. regulation requires that the front door remain open at all times, and during the summer months the oppressive heat— temperatures are comparable to Washington, D.C.—renders the air conditioning units possessed by some *kōban* useless.

Often billboards are located outside *kōban* and *chūzaisho* on which posters of "wanted" persons are pinned up. The drab gray cement of most police boxes is sometimes brightened by flowers or bowls of fruit, though this is more characteristic of the residential police boxes. Quite often food is delivered to the *kōban* by a local restaurant; otherwise, officers may bring something from home. When officers go out for a meal, they do not wear uniforms as it is against police regulations to do so, and most officers, sensitive of citizens who have not forgotten the arrogance of officers prior to the Second World War, prefer not to appear in uniform other than in an official capacity.

Appreciating grass roots police services in Japan requires some understanding of the organizational structure behind the policeman "on the beat." The rank structure of police in Japan is:

Police Superintendent Supervisor
Chief Police Superintendent
Senior Police Superintendent
Police Superintendent
Police Inspector
Assistant Police Inspector
Police Sergeant
Senior Policeman
Policeman

At the M.P.D., a Superintendent General is in charge. This is the only such position in the entire country, reflecting the "queen bee" status of this department. Only the Commissioner General of the National Police Agency ranks above the chief of the M.P.D. and he, of course, is in charge of all police services for the nation. One key ingredient of the national system is that all officers at the rank of Senior Police Superintendent and above are considered to be national public servants in the employ of the National Police Agency. They are appointed by the National Public Safety Commission. At the M.P.D., police officials of the rank of Superintendent and below are local public officials who are appointed and dismissed by the Superintendent General in consultation with the Tokyo Public Safety Commission. In addition to the National Public Safety Commission, each prefecture has its own Public Safety Commission.

The Tsukiji Police Station

Before visiting the mini-police stations, or *kōban*, in a particular area, I met with the chief who had jurisdiction over that district. The chief of the Tsukiji station—my first area—was an affable, older, graying man who wore single stars on his lapels that indicated his rank of senior superintendent. The ninety-five police stations of the M.P.D. are headed by either superintendents or senior superintendents. He was courteous and seemed eager to accommodate me. Within moments of my arrival, tea was served, as is customary, and we were joined by several assistants, including the station's full-time interpreter. Officially the station is known as the Tsukiji station but the area it encompasses is popularly known as the Ginza. The Ginza, unlike most other districts, has thousands of foreign tourists daily, and it is necessary to have a full-time police interpreter available.

These visits with station chiefs were not merely courtesies, but provided opportunities for them to brief me on the characteristics of their operations and for me to ask questions. What was particularly intriguing about the Ginza was the fact that within these 2.5 square kilometers (about 1 square mile) over 3,000 pubs, restaurants, and other "public morals businesses," as the chief called them, plied their trade. Only 9,877 households with 23,358 residents exist in this area, a reflection of its commercial character. While the number of 23,358 residents is low, some 200,000 individuals work here and 500,000 people, including visitors and shoppers, flow in and out on any given day. Ten police boxes operate under the Tsukiji station, and total personnel number around 400. The gigantic Tsukiji fish market involves around 70,000 persons daily, mostly buyers and sellers. A private security force is employed in the market area, but the M.P.D. patrols the perimeter and the rest of the Tsukiji/Ginza area.

During the early stages of my study, I began by asking foot patrolmen as well as supervisors about the types of situations they encountered in routine police work. I was particularly interested in the frequency and severity of violent crime. The Tsukiji police chief stated that, "Citizens rarely use weapons. While they may punch or strike out, it's almost unheard of for guns to be used— even the use of knives is unusual." Domestic violence or, more specifically, husband–wife fights, whatever their actual incidence, are rarely reported to police. When pressed on this subject, officers, including several who became personal friends, conceded that there are such disputes but went on to explain that both the husbands and the wives are too embarrassed to report them. They maintained that there is little physical violence among couples. More common are complaints about excessive noise from a neighbor or unpaid loans to a friend or acquaintance. While officers on small town forces in the United States sometimes engage in this type of work, it is rare in larger cities. In the case of Tsukiji, this personal and financial counseling was rare at the main station, with only forty cases for the previous year, but, I was told, it was more common at the several *kōban* in the district.

As in the United States, in Japan police have an emergency telephone number (110). At the Communications Command Center, in the headquarters of the Tokyo Metropolitan Police Department, 530,000 calls were received for the entire city during 1979. Operators sitting at large video consoles refer many calls to the different police stations, including the Tsukiji station. One call was received every twenty-four seconds at the headquarters facility, but, as with emergency numbers in the United States, many calls have little to do with law enforcement. For instance, calls from emotionally disturbed persons or simple routine requests for general information are often received. M.P.D. officials estimated that about one call per month was received that had to do with a "hostage" type of situation.

Nationally, one "110" call was received every 11.4 seconds, and a total of 2,766,793 calls were received during 1979. This represented a 3.5 percent increase over the previous year. Emergency calls automatically go through the Communications Center of each prefectural headquarters. Calls peak during the 10 P.M. to midnight period. The National Police Agency reported the following frequency ranking for emergency calls:

1. Traffic accidents (26.3 percent).
2. People offering information of different types, e.g., calls to give information on a "wanted" person (11.6 percent).
3. People calling a second time on the same matter (10.8 percent).
4. Inquiries to the police for some type of information (10.2 percent).
5. Reports on "victimization" penal code crimes (9.6 percent).
6. Requests for the protection of a drunk (7.7 percent).
7. Requests for police to take some action (6.3 percent).
8. Reports on quarrels and disputes (5.4 percent).
9. Reports on sick or injured persons (2.7 percent).
10. Reports on runaway or missing children (2.4 percent).
11. Reports on fires (1.6 percent).
12. Wrong numbers (1.5 percent).
13. Reports on violations of other laws (0.7 percent).
14. Miscellaneous (3.2 percent).

At the Ginza station they recorded 2,400 "110" calls for 1979. Most of these were not complaints involving serious criminal offenses but reflected the general pattern of calls received at the Communications Command Center: 500 calls concerning traffic accidents; 400 calls involving parking complaints; 200 calls regarding drunks; and just 100 calls involving fights and disputes. Interestingly, there were almost as many reports of items "found" (approximately 4,000) as reports on items "lost" (approximately 6,000). One suspects that the ratio would be slightly different for American cities.

Tokyo M.P.D. headquarters officials explained that each patrol officer is responsible on the average for routine visits to 450 households or commercial establishments. For my first such visit I accompanied a middle-aged sergeant to interview the manager of a new ten-story commercial building, just three blocks from the Sukiyabashi police box. Asked about crime or vandalism, he said there was none to report for the first ten months of operation. His only complaint was that drunks occasionally slept at night under the overhanging roof of the building. A card is filled out by the officer on each of the residences or businesses visited, and it is filed at the police box (see Figures 1a and 1b).

A two-page pamphlet has been prepared to tell police recruits how to approach these "routine visits." Entitled "Guidance on Home Visits," it provides specific suggestions on "etiquette," conversational ploys, and a variety of "dos" and "don'ts":

I. Etiquette
   1. Dress properly and neatly.
   2. Knock on the door or ring doorbell before entering.
   3. Do not peep in windows or touch articles such as decorations at the entrance.
   4. When offered a chair or *zabuton* (cushion), sit down and greet the person properly.
   5. If a woman receives you, keep the door open unless she asks you to close it.

II. Communication
   1. Offer appropriate greetings, indicating why you have come. If you are visiting the house for the first time, introduce yourself. For those who are not familiar with routine visits, explain and ask for their cooperation.
   2. Select appropriate words. Make your speech clear with a choice of language appropriate to the person you are addressing. You may use the local dialect if there is one in your area.

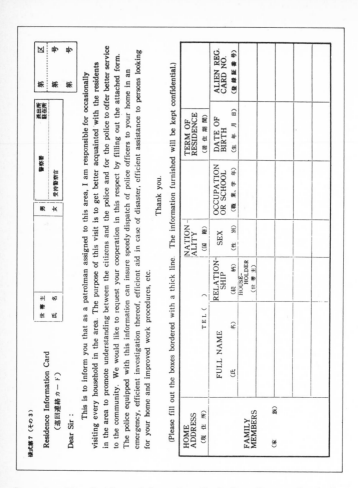

Figure 1a. The Residence Information Card (for alien residents) that policemen fill out on regular visits to households

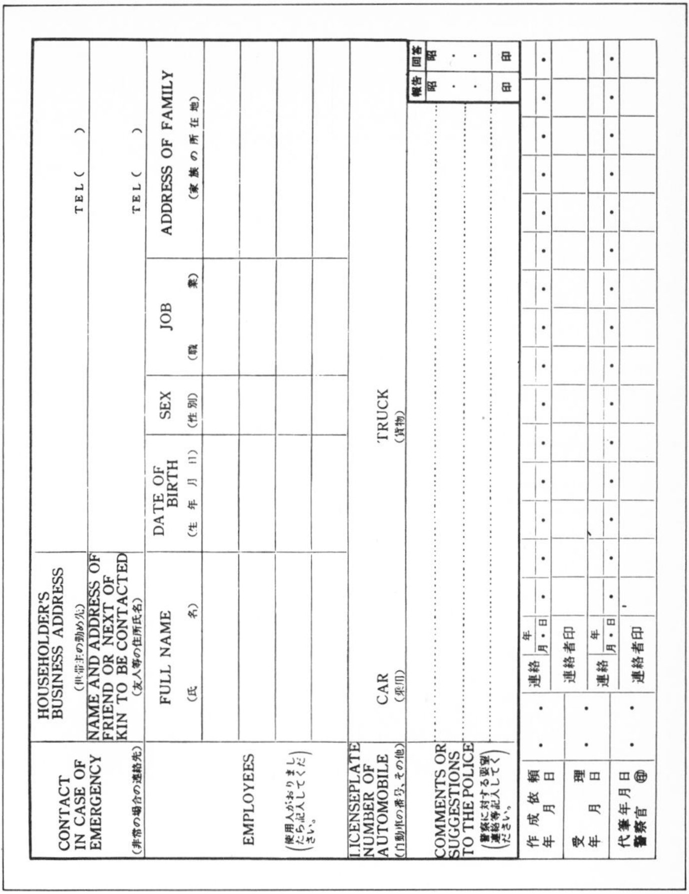

CONTACT IN CASE OF EMERGENCY (非常の場合の連絡先)	HOUSEHOLDER'S BUSINESS ADDRESS (甲帯主の勤め先) TEL ( )
	NAME AND ADDRESS OF FRIEND OR NEXT OF KIN TO BE CONTACTED (友人等の住所氏名) TEL ( )

	FULL NAME (氏 名)	DATE OF BIRTH (生 年 月 日)	SEX (性 別)	JOB (職 業)	ADDRESS OF FAMILY (家族の所在地)
EMPLOYEES (使用人がおりましたらご記入ください)					

LICENSEPLATE NUMBER OF AUTOMOBILE (自動車の番号、その他)	CAR (乗用)	TRUCK (貨物)

COMMENTS OR SUGGESTIONS TO THE POLICE (警察に対する要望・意見等記入して下さい)

作 成 依 頼 年 月 日	·	·	連絡 月・日	年	·
受 月 理 日	·	·	連絡者印
代筆年月日 警察官印	·	·	連絡 月・日	年	·
			連絡者印

報告 回答
昭 · · 昭 印
昭 · · 昭 印

Figure 1b. The reverse of the Residence Information Card

III. Note the Occasion

　1. Avoid ceremonial occasions, when there are guests or when people are occupied with work.

　2. When there is no one at home and contact is difficult, ask the neighbors when the family might be at home in order to carry out the routine visit.

IV. Note the Content of the Conversation

　1. Speak of familiar, interesting matters and make the conversation easy to understand.

　2. Do not say things that may hurt the feelings of the residents.

　3. Avoid rumors concerning neighbors and political topics.

Officers have varying levels of interest in making the "routine visits," and older officers who are more experienced and have more poise seem to enjoy it more than younger men. Increasingly, there are instances in which these visits—not authorized by law but sustained by tradition—result in rejection by the resident, and younger officers occasionally seem uncomfortable, if not intimidated, through these encounters.

One is struck by the very low-keyed nature of police patrol work in Japan. Generally patrol police in Japan present a lower profile and engage in less "muscle flexing" with the public than do American officers. In Ginza, at the Sukiyabashi police box, which is perhaps the busiest of all in Japan, one does not sense an air of emergency that typifies so many United States inner-city police stations. While on some Friday nights there are drunken fights, generally there is no bloodshed of the type Americans have become familiar with. Accordingly, the policeman on the beat, or in his *kōban*, seems more relaxed than his American counterpart.

At Sukiyabashi, several officers remain inside, engaged in administrative work and processing complaints, while one or two officers stand alertly outside the *kōban*, demonstrating their receptiveness to inquiries and other matters. By far the most common request is for directions. Because most Japanese streets have no names and are numbered in a confusing way, giving directions to those unfamiliar with the area is a common task for Japanese police. In a central area of a large city, it is often the major task.

The Sukiyabashi police box, one of the busiest in downtown Tokyo.

Surprisingly, during my interviews with *kōban* police I rarely encountered an officer who had ever drawn his gun. After approximately a month of the field study, having asked the question perhaps fifty times, I stopped inquiring directly about police use of firearms. One officer stated that when he had been called to a bank robbery in progress, in which the person inside was suspected of being armed, he had drawn his weapon but had not fired it. An officer's response at the Sukiyabashi police box was typical. He said that he had never drawn his weapon and, as far as he knew, not one officer stationed at his police box had drawn a weapon during the two years he had been assigned to that location. Despite the bright lights, noise, and huge crowds that remind one of American cities, police in Japan confront only a fraction of the violent crime that American officers encounter. Henry Kamm, in an article for *The New York Times*, described several evenings spent with police in the Ikebukuro section of Tokyo. He observed that the area was a "teeming district of bars, cheap eating places, porno shops, Turkish baths that serve as a cover for prostitution, and two dozen love hotels where rooms can be rented by the hour." Despite this picture of a Japanese-style "Times Square," he says:

> No crime was reported, no complaints were lodged, and no arrests were made. The only suspects questioned were men pushing bicycles that, despite arousing patrolmen's suspicion, proved to be owned and registered by the suspects. The only harsh treatment meted out was by an angry mother coming to reclaim her two small daughters who, instead of doing their homework, went in search of their father at a game parlor but lost sight of him.[3]

The first problem encountered by police during the afternoon of my first *kōban* visit involved the report of a bicycle theft. A man who appeared to be a businessman in his thirties claimed that his bicycle had been locked but nonetheless had been stolen. It is a popular myth that Japanese do not lock the doors to their homes or attempt to secure other articles, such as bicycles, but in Tokyo, despite its low crime rates, many people do take such precautions. I was told, however, that people in rural areas still do not bother to lock their doors. Even if they lock their front doors, they often will not have made the rest of the house secure by locking the windows. Owners of new bicycles in rural areas usually lock them up, but older bikes are often not secured.

Visits and observation of police activities at various *kōban* in the Ginza were informative in a number of ways. A visit to the Odawarachō police box brought to light one aspect of the supervisory process. On that occasion I happened to meet the assistant police inspector who was making a routine visit as part of his circuit. He informed me that he traveled by bicycle to all ten police boxes in the Ginza offering "guidance" to recruits or newly assigned personnel. In addition, he was responsible for overseeing the activity of each police box in the district, and, in case of a robbery or other emergency, he had to be available to coordinate the various police boxes. In short, he functioned as a liaison between the police station and the *kōban*. For each of the four shifts, a different officer assumed these liaison and supervisory functions.

This assistant inspector's explanation of why Japanese police administrators do not employ many women officers at the *kōban* would not have pleased American policewomen. "It would be difficult, lots of walking, a lot of physical strain, working alone at night." This remark was not offered in a critical tone, but it reflects a general stereotype regarding the role of women. In the forty-seven prefectures, there were 3,000 policewomen, 2,900 traffic patrolwomen, and 800 female "guidance" officers during 1977.[4] Women continue to be treated as second-class citizens within the labor market. While women's liberation enjoyed a brief period of popularity a number of years ago (apparently in imitation of events in the United States), the movement has not yet developed deep roots. Many college-educated women complain of severely limited opportunities for securing attractive jobs. Once hired, prospects for promotion are much less than for men. During 1979, the average monthly wage for women in Japan was ¥158,825 ($690), and for men, ¥289,052 ($1,256).[5]

My experiences at these first police boxes taught me some things about the general structure of the force that might have been difficult to learn from direct questions. In fact, who would and who would not answer my questions was in itself instructive. Lower-ranking officers questioned on general policy matters occasionally appeared perplexed at the inquiries. Initially, I wondered if they were attempting to deflect controversy by giving short, superficial responses. However, somewhat later an alternative hypothesis emerged, namely that they had not concerned themselves with the subject; it was a matter for "higher-ups" to decide. For example, I asked a senior policeman at the Shintomichō Ekimae *kōban* if he thought it was necessary to visit all residential and commer-

A police box of modern design in the Ginza area of downtown Tokyo (*left*), and another (*below*) that is more typical in its appearance.

Police boxes enable the police to be readily available for giving directions (*left*), and for consultation (*above*). Names of police boxes are usually in Japanese, but they may also be in English if the vicinity has a lot of tourists (*below*).

cial buildings twice a year. He replied, "They've decided it," "they" being the police administration.

To counter this reluctance to give clear answers, whether due to anxiety over the prying of a foreigner, or to deference to superiors, I tried to create a low-keyed, relaxed atmosphere at the police boxes. At the outset of a visit to a new *kōban*, I mentioned that I was willing to talk with them about any aspect of American life that might be of interest. In addition, I had pictures of my family with me and frequently produced them, particularly in conversations with older officers who were often family men themselves. By indicating openness to their concerns, they understood that my research interests did not preclude discussions of other subjects.

On the whole these tactics succeeded, perhaps largely because the atmosphere at the *kōban* was naturally relaxed. Ten years ago this task might have been more difficult: the atmosphere at some of these police boxes was more tense in the late sixties when radical student groups were aggressive. Many confrontations took place between police and students, and the police were called in to quell riots at the prestigious Tokyo University and elsewhere. One officer recounted how they were required systematically to search the immediate premises of the *kōban* every fifteen minutes for explosives.

Interviews at *kōban* were not the only means of learning about the "grass roots" police. I also spent some time on patrol with officers. One evening around midnight, accompanying a motorized patrol, a huge underground garage was checked. On the three levels, over seventy men were loitering. Some were drunks, others were just down and out. One fellow, despite his unshaven, skid row appearance, claimed he made ¥150,000 ($652) a month by playing *pachinko*, a popular Japanese pinball game, the prizes of which are often surreptitiously exchanged for cash. Gambling for money is prohibited in Japan, but the sergeant explained that prosecution takes place only when the offense is directly observed by police. There were brief, amiable exchanges between the sergeant and several men, and no attempt was made to roust any of them from their overnight lodging.

The visit to the Tsukiji fish market police box was a fascinating and enjoyable experience despite the fact that it started before sunrise. It is necessary to arrive very early in order to capture the spirit of the market bargaining, which is in full swing by 4 A.M. The police box is located at the entrance to the market area. The older officer on duty reported that the area, which includes over two thousand shops, is relatively crime-free, with only occasional reports of pickpockets. Two or three complaints a day are received. In earlier years, there were problems with "toughs," who would occasionally get into knife fights, but the shop owners banded together to get rid of these undesirables. The main job for officers assigned to this *kōban* is giving crime prevention information and making routine visits to the shop owners.

This seasoned officer, like many others, reported a reduction in the level of citizen cooperation over the years. He felt that young people, in particular, were less responsive to police officer contacts, and sometimes did not even answer when he asked a question. He said that, "Before and right after the Second World War, the police were both respected and feared, but today some people are tempted to abolish the *kōban* system because of the decreased level of cooperation. I believe it should be maintained, but patience is required." The changing nature of citizen attitudes toward the police proved to be a recurrent theme, and often *kōban* officers would raise the issue themselves, demonstrating that it was a major problem.

Much later, an officer patrolling the Hongō area of Tokyo found a good way of summarizing the changes he had witnessed over the ten years of his service: "They used to treat us like members of the family and invite us in for coffee or tea; today that would be unthinkable." This problem of the weakening of ties between citizens and police in urban areas is of concern to police administrators, but to some it seems the inevitable product of modern industrialization. No clearcut official strategy to attack this problem appears to have been formulated; officers are left to find their own solutions.

The most common police vehicles: (*below*) motorcycle police stand in front of one of the buses used by the riot police (*kidōtai*); the patrol car (*below*); and (*left*) the ubiquitous bicycle used by street police patrolling out of police boxes.

Policing Tokyo's Outlying Areas: Shitaya, Seijō, Akabane, Motofuji, and Sanya

The outlying police station areas I studied are for the most part very urban in character. Though unlike the Ginza, with its tourist attractions, high-priced restaurants, glittering shops, and smart nightclubs, among these "suburban" urban areas there is a certain similarity. They are on average forty to sixty minutes by train from the heart of the city, each is quite commercial, and all blend readily into the seemingly endless bustling sea of Metropolitan Tokyo. The one exception is the district served by the Seijō police station, where one finds the homes of middle-income and wealthy citizens—a kind of Japanese Westchester or Westport, with the qualification that houses and yards are considerably smaller.

The Shitaya Police Station

The demands on police administrators are quite different in this older section of Tokyo, which has approximately 240 personnel assigned to it. In the early days of the city, when it was still called Edo, a considerable number of politicians lived in this district. Many families can trace their ancestry back several generations, and traditional festivals are still enthusiastically celebrated. Craftsmen and intellectuals also live in Shitaya, and they have contributed to continuing economic stability, according to officials. While there is a great deal of commercial activity, relationships between police and citizens are closer here than in the Ginza or in the areas of Tokyo with a more transient population. Police chiefs are in an excellent position to comment on variations within the city because superintendents and senior superintendents are rotated approximately every two years. The chief at this station in Shitaya mentioned that, "Notwithstanding the fact that this is a city, people here do have an affection for their neighborhood." One consequence of the closer relationship between police and citizens is the increased activity of crime prevention associations, which total forty-nine in number. These are organized according to district and include "housewife associations," according to Shitaya police personnel. A social scientist at the National Research Institute of Police Science, the research arm of the National Police

Agency, mentioned that the more conservative elements in the community, including shopkeepers and others who have much to gain from a close relationship with police, provide the backbone of crime prevention activity.

These relationships and associations seem to pay off with impressively low crime rates. The chief and his staff noted that while there are occasional burglaries in Shitaya, these tend to be of houses, occurring when the occupants are out. Armed robbery is extraordinarily rare, and these officials said that there had been no bank robberies in their district in the previous five-year period. Moreover, there were only two or three homicides per year for this entire station area.

These results notwithstanding, interviews with *kōban* police personnel in a variety of Japanese cities indicated that officers do not know their neighborhoods thoroughly, despite the aid from the neighborhood associations. Several officers who had read Bayley, usually in the Japanese translation, disagreed with him on this point. At one *kōban* in Shitaya, officers said it is possible to know a neighborhood thoroughly only when residents move very infrequently. Police record basic information—the names of residents, current employment, etc.—on cards filed in the *kōban*, but in many neighborhoods people move too frequently for officers to keep accurate records from the "routine visits." For instance, at this *kōban*, whose jurisdiction includes approximately thirty-five hundred households and businesses, the two officers on duty said the turnover was around one thousand every two years or so. Most of those who move are families living in the apartment complexes that have recently proliferated in a number of areas of the city.

Despite the crowded living conditions in Tokyo, the officers claimed that only about five calls a year about family quarrels are received at their police boxes, and inevitably the dispute has subsided by the time the officers arrive. As noted earlier, the Japanese are reluctant to call the police about domestic disputes, and when the police are called embarrassment seems to put an end to the quarrel before officers arrive.

The Shitaya police station had the following specialists assigned to it: five detectives, three crime prevention officers, five public safety officers (who handle prostitution, drug enforcement, and firearms violations), and five juvenile officers.

During my visits to Shitaya, I learned of another difference between the work of Japanese and American police, namely, that the Japanese police rarely go to court. Information they gather on a criminal case is turned over to a prosecutor, and the court does not require their personal appearance. The prosecutor's written statement is usually sufficient.

One of the highlights of the field study conducted at Shitaya was the visit to the "Single Men's Kendo and Judo Tournament." Kendo is a form of fencing using a bamboo sword. Officers, outfitted in medieval-looking robes and wearing face shields, utter war cries as combat is joined. We started with a rousing send-off by the chief at an early morning ceremonial gathering in the upstairs gym of the Shitaya police station, which included the beating of a huge drum, a saké toast, and a "pep" talk by the chief. The contestants then traveled twenty minutes to the site of the tournament, where they met teams from eight other police stations. After a brief warmup period, there was another short ceremony for all the participants. One of the reasons one rarely encounters an overweight Japanese police officer is that, as mentioned earlier, all officers are required to take either judo or kendo, and promotions at the lower levels require proficiency in these sports. Physical exercise is continued by most police long after the required years of training are over. Moreover, foot and bicycle patrols are still far more common than motorized patrols, and this contributes to the trim appearance of most personnel.

The Seijō Police Station

While the problem of eyewitness testimony is not peculiar to the Seijō station, I have included it at this point since the subject was raised at this station for the first time. The problems of eyewitness testimony are due, in general, to the inherent unreliability of eyewitnesses, but the problem is compounded by poorly developed procedures for conducting lineups and photo arrays by the police. In the United States the issue has received an increasing amount of attention from the courts and social scientists in recent years (see Elizabeth Loftus, 1979, and L. Craig Parker, 1980), but a great deal of work remains to be done.

The situation is worse in Japan, where relatively few precautions are taken in this delicate matter. Photo arrays are conducted far more often than corporeal, or "in person," identifications, which experts have regarded as being superior (see Patrick Wall, 1965). Research into the administration of photo arrays has demonstrated that it is such a subtle process that officers who administer them can easily and unwittingly bias the witness. Many cases are on record (e.g., see Edwin Borchard, 1932) in both Britain and the United States in which innocent parties have been convicted by confident but mistaken witnesses. Potentially even more prejudicial than the use of photo arrays is the use of "show-ups"—an arrangement in which a witness encounters a suspect in a one-on-one situation (sometimes face-to-face and sometimes through a one-way window). The U.S. Supreme Court has ruled against these and other circumstances that generate prejudice against the suspect. Nevertheless, "show-ups" and other similar techniques are apparently common in Japan.

Ministry of Justice officials and police administrators indicated that lineups are rarely employed in Japan. A lineup involves inserting a suspect into a group of individuals who are not so unlike the suspect as to draw the attention of the witness to him, and the witness is usually offered the opportunity to view the lineup through a one-way window. In place of a lineup, one official at the Seijō police station explained that "photos are used first, before the confrontation between witness and suspect is arranged, and then the witness is allowed to observe the suspect through a type of one-way window. If you have to arrest the criminal quickly (for example, if a series of thefts has occurred), then the witnesses are allowed to observe the suspect directly . . . while their memories are fresh." These "show-ups" present serious problems since, among other things, the witness may be recalling the photo of the person he identified previously rather than the actual image of the person. (See, for example, my discussion in *Legal Psychology: Eyewitness Testimony, Jury Behavior*.) Japanese procedures seem to reflect a lower level of concern for the rights of the accused.

On several occasions I asked public prosecutors and police officials how a judge—there are no jury trials in Japan—would be able to determine if the eyewitness identification process has been tainted. The consistent answer was that it is entirely up to the judge to make a determination of the accuracy and reliability of the eyewitness identification. Obviously, there is no way for even the most conscientious judge to obtain a complete and exact idea of procedures undertaken by the police and prosecutors.

A "montage" device—which allows a technician to create a composite facial likeness of a suspect with the help of a witness—is also employed by the Tokyo Metropolitan Police Department headquarters personnel. This is a more sophisticated form of the "Identi-Kit" device commonly used by police in the United States.

The primarily residential area covered by the Seijō police station is ten times larger than that covered by the Shitaya station, and the main problems confronting police are somewhat different. The Seijō administrators stated that house burglaries are the main concern. The network of community groups and crime prevention associations is weaker due to the life-styles of these upper-income families, and an increase of twenty percent in house burglaries over the previous year had been recorded for this area. Experienced burglars were primarily responsible, with one culprit having a record of seventeen prior arrests. Interestingly, none of those apprehended was armed even with a knife.

Police patrols and visits to *kōban* revealed typical minor problems: resident complaints of large trucks using a quiet, narrow, non-commercial street; an annoying "Peeping Tom"; and several bicycle thefts.

I was fortunate that there were several officers with whom I became personal friends. I visited their homes, ate with them, played tennis with them, and visited nightclubs and jazz coffee shops with them in the Ginza, Shinjuku, Harajuku, and other places. This was not only a very pleasant experience in its own right but offered an opportunity to check on various matters and confirm or refute certain points raised in the course of the field research. One patrol sergeant was particularly helpful. He was a college graduate, exceptionally bright and personable, and was familiar not only with Bayley's work but the work of other American criminologists. One evening, he made the following comments:

> Policemen who are ambitious do a lot of questioning of citizens. For example, when patrolling the streets, it is fairly easy to do. If someone has a light out on his bicycle, he can be stopped and rather easily persuaded (if he is initially evasive) to give basic information about himself—what his name is, where he is from, where he is going. He will cooperate, although reluctantly at times. I might do this six or seven times a night.

This is a prime example, along with the routine family visits, of how Japanese police penetrate, as David Bayley states, deeper into the community than do their American counterparts. The reasons are obvious. In the United States a citizen would no doubt loudly voice his "rights" if confronted by the kind of police behavior just described.

Occasionally, one hears of complaints from foreigners who are offended by what they consider the audaciousness of the Japanese police. A professional woman employee of a U.S. government office in Tokyo offered the following episode as an example. This Japanese-American speaks fluent Japanese and has lived in Tokyo for a number of years. She stated that she and an acquaintance, a male American scholar, were stopped by two men in business suits while headed for lunch in the Akasaka area of Tokyo. The officers inquired where the couple were going, to which she responded by asking who they were. The men immediately furnished their police identification cards. She then asked why they had been stopped, but they did not reply. The officers repeated their questions and the woman reluctantly replied that they were headed for lunch. One officer smirked and again repeated his question, to which she angrily retorted, "To lunch!" The police then asked about the nature of their relationship and in the process discovered that her companion was not carrying his alien registration card, which all foreigners are legally required to have on them at all times. The officers then asked the couple to accompany them to the nearest police box, despite the woman's protest that the man's alien registration card was easily accessible—a three-minute walk to his office. At the police box, the man was asked the purpose of his being in Japan, and he informed the officers that he was seeking employment. They responded that there was no way that they could be assured of the veracity of his statement. The American visitor was then asked to provide further identification and to sign a form letter of apology. In addition, he had to promise to report back with his alien registration card. This incident illustrates the ease with which Japanese police can make inquiries at their own discretion (a privilege that would be the envy of American police), and the indignant and angry feelings of foreigners subjected to such tactics.

Courts in the United States continue to be sensitive to possible rights violations by police. In early 1982, the U.S. Supreme Court ruled that a California law allowing police to arrest vagrants was unconstitutional. A vagrant in California law was defined as one "who loiters or wanders from place to place without apparent reason or business, and who refuses to identify himself when asked by a police officer." While a number of states continue to have such laws, many others have struck them down. The key issue becomes to what degree police may detain, question or otherwise impede a private citizen when they lack "probable cause" to make an arrest.

The Akabane Police Station

The Akabane station area covers approximately twenty-five square kilometers (about ten square miles) and is located at the northern end of the Tokyo Metropolitan Police Department's jurisdiction, bordering Saitama Prefecture. The low-income housing projects found here have somewhat higher crime rates than the surrounding areas, but it is crime against property and is not violent— bicycle theft, petty larceny, and similar offenses.

In Akabane, officers generally expressed concern about a recent increase in burglaries of homes and a rash of bank robberies.

A sampling of the signs and posters commonly seen outside police boxes. The poster with a popular singer urging young people to behave well both on the road and off is flanked by a banner exhorting motorcyclists to wear helmets. At the extreme right is a board showing traffic casualty figures. Boards with "Wanted" persons (*below*) may be inside or outside the police box.

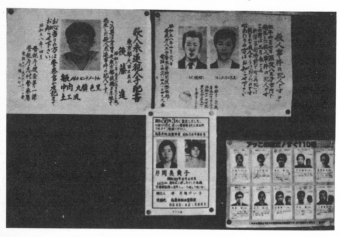

Concerning changes in the nature of police work over recent years, the problem of dealing with citizens intent on expressing their "rights" was once again voiced. This issue, in various forms, was raised by more officers during the field study than any other. One officer put it this way: "Before, people were obedient to their seniors, but now you have to explain before asking a person to do something."

A discussion with one officer concerning domestic disputes was revealing. Asked about their frequency and how they are handled, he commented:

> We receive such a call about once a week, but usually it's quietened down by the time we arrive. We are ready to protect ourselves when we walk in, but usually there is little violence between the husband and wife—rather, it may be directed at an object, like breaking a window. Only once or twice a year do we have to break up the fight and often it's because they are drunk. If it is necessary to intervene, our training in judo or kendo is sufficient.

Concerning wife beating, the officer suspected that there was some but that unless the wife wanted a divorce, there was not much use in reporting it. Furthermore, he noted that there was a tradition that prevented the enforcing of laws related to crimes within the family.

In the Akabane and Motofuji *kōban*, and in fact all over Japan, I saw posters with slogans. A cynical American policeman might view these with disdain, but they seem to have real meaning to Japanese police. Sometimes officers submit their own slogans to M.P.D. headquarters, and these may appear later in a published circular. Some *kōban* police even repeat these slogans before starting a shift. One "permanent" poster spotted on several occasions said, "To have good contact with people and show understanding, to get the confidence of people." Another poster declared, "Don't take it out of the holster, don't put your finger on the trigger, don't point it at people." Occasionally, a "goal for the month" poster was observed. One said, "Try hard to stay in good condition mentally and physically," while another exhorted, "Try your best to be responsible and maintain a sense of duty." A more elaborate poster spotted on the back room wall of one *kōban* was entitled "Five Goals."

1. Try to meet each person honestly and try to gain the respect and understanding of the local community.
2. Try to melt into or fit into the community by taking the initiative and grasping the area of your jurisdiction.
3. Try actively and constructively to question people on the street in order to prevent crime and make arrests.
4. Be alert and be nimble in terms of organizing your activities in order to solve each case as quickly as possible.
5. Work properly, correctly, and with dignity. Be fully alert in preventing any crime or accident.

The Motofuji Police Station

This station's jurisdiction includes the main campus of Tokyo University, but officers are quick to point out that it would take a serious emergency for an officer to dare to enter the campus. Tokyo University was the scene of some pitched battles between police and students during the late 1960s; it is now required that the chief of the Motofuji station be a Tokyo University graduate. The chief at the time of my visit was a graduate of the law department in his mid-thirties, who was a student at the time the police entered the campus. An agreement now exists that the president of the university will consult with police officials before any officers are allowed on campus. This young chief was particularly receptive to questions and was extremely helpful in explaining the problems of policing this area. A member of the elite police, he, like his colleagues, had been rotated through various assignments and had recently left a post on the northernmost island, Hokkaido. His rank was superintendent. Officers under his command noted that he placed great emphasis on family visits.

One interesting piece of information that emerged from visits to *kōban* in the Motofuji area came from an officer about to be transferred to a prison. He commented that he would still be a police officer and that he was doing this to further his career aspirations as a detective. He explained that this prison exposure to "see how criminals are handled" would expand his understanding of the justice process, and he added that the policy had existed for around twenty years.

During a brief visit to the "Hongō Crossing" police box, just a few blocks from the Tokyo University campus, it was clear that giving directions was the main activity; over two hundred inquiries are answered daily. University students occasionally tease an officer, but the violent clashes between police and students common in the late 1960s no longer occur.

Some competition exists among the four different shifts of the patrol division stationed at the Motofuji station as regards the number of traffic violations recorded, robberies solved, and so on, although investigations of the latter crime are pretty much in the hands of the detective division. Traffic enforcement is a controversial subject since administrators are concerned that too rigorous an enforcement of traffic laws leads to the alienation of citizens, but it was the judgment of the senior policeman that the competition between the four shifts had more advantages than disadvantages: "It increases the individual's incentive to do a good job and it betters the team spirit—it peps up the whole morale."

At an average *kōban* there are approximately five hundred households assigned to each officer for the purpose of the routine family visits. Sometimes officers are selected to do the residential survey exclusively. Officers at one *kōban* admitted that the transient population presented serious problems in terms of knowledge of the neighborhood. One officer noted that just one homicide had occurred in the area during the previous year. A woman was murdered at a porno shop while watching the store for the owner. The assailant was arrested after an eight-month investigation.

Policing Sanya

This lower-class section of Tokyo has many transients, and police officials point it out as perhaps the most crime-ridden area of the metropolis. It is a small, skid row district of Tokyo in which criminal offenders often attempt to elude authorities by disappearing among the many jobless transients. Residents live in run-down, single men's rooming houses and hotels.

In late 1981, J. Laurie reported for an ABC News special report on the plight of one Sanya resident. A former businessman, then in his sixties, he had been fired by Mitsui Trust for diverting funds into a loan, which he had been unable to repay. Relatives ridiculed him and his wife divorced him. Ashamed, he sought shelter in Sanya, where people do not inquire about one's background, and had lived there alone for half of his life.

I paid a visit to this area accompanied by my interpreter on a late afternoon in the early autumn of 1980. Groups of disheveled men loitered around the *kōban* area. This police box, like most others, is a very small, inconspicuous, two-story building with a drab facade. A young inspector of the National Police Agency had joined us that day, and we decided at the last moment to make this stop after having visited the nearby Asakusa Juvenile Counseling Center. An inspector in his late forties received us in the rather crowded space on the second floor of the *kōban*, a small, open room with several other officers seated at desks. (It is common practice for section chiefs and supervisors, in business and government as well as police work, to sit in an open area with their subordinates.) The chief was friendly and explained that men in the area contracted for daily work and that this lack of stability and the emotional difficulties that accompany it contribute to the excessive drinking and fighting that are common.

Later, wandering through the side streets of the neighborhood, one older man reached out to touch my female interpreter. On the whole though, aside from this one feeble gesture, for a neighborhood considered to be among the most dangerous in Japan, it pales in comparison with neighborhoods in Brooklyn, the Bronx, or Manhattan. For that matter, the inner-city areas of most American cities appear far more run-down and menacing than this district. Most urban areas of Japan are relatively clean and pleasant to live in, by American standards. Police, even in this area, are not deeply concerned about the safety of a foreigner walking through the narrow streets. While a mugging or purse snatching might occur, a serious assault or a homicide would be extremely unlikely.

Bayley notes that because many of the residents of Sanya were too poor to own watches, the local *kōban* erected a large, illuminated clock to assist men in reporting to work on time. A message board on which were posted weather reports and notices to individuals from friends or family members was also constructed. This, however, is hardly a new service of the Japanese police, since Westney (1982) notes that as early as 1884 the police were posting daily weather reports near the station houses and *kōban* as a means of inducing the public to read police bulletins.

This survey of police box activity in Tokyo will be contrasted in the next chapter with the duties and functions of police assigned to *chūzaisho*, or residential police boxes, in the country areas.

NOTES

1. Keishichō, *Metropolitan Police Department* (Tokyo, 1980), p. 2.
2. E. Westney, "The Emulation of Western Organizations in Meiji Japan: The Case of Paris Prefecture of Police and the Keishi-Cho," *The Journal of Japanese Studies*, 8, No. 2, 1982, p. 35.
3. H. Kamm, "In Tokyo, A Raucous Honky-Tonk Area That Has No Crime," *The New York Times*, July 22, 1981, p. A3.
4. Foreign Press Center, *Japan: A Pocket Guide* (Tokyo: Foreign Press Center, 1979).
5. Statistics Bureau, *Statistical Handbook of Japan* (Tokyo: Prime Minister's Office, 1980).

Figure 2

Police Organization (National Level)

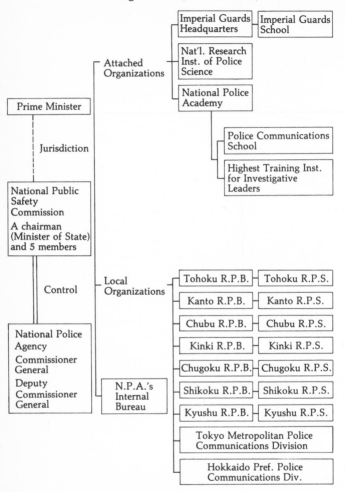

Remarks: R.P.B. (Regional Police Bureau)
R.P.S. (Regional Police School)

Chapter 4

THE HOKKAIDO PREFECTURAL POLICE

The Hokkaido Setting

Hokkaido ranks second to Honshu in size among Japan's five major islands, accounting for 85,513 square kilometers out of Japan's total 377,643 square kilometers. While primarily rural in character, with the major activities being dairy farming, fishing, and forestry, industrial growth has taken place in cities like Sapporo, Hakodate, and Asahikawa. Hokkaido is one of the few regions of Japan without mountains that is not densely populated—it has fewer than ninety-nine persons per square mile, and a stroll through Sapporo's streets might remind one of a northern United States city like Minneapolis or a Canadian city like Edmonton. Boulevards are wide and laid out in a grid pattern, and there are many new highrise office buildings and hotels. There was a spurt of new growth, including the creation of a huge underground mall, at the time of the 1972 Winter Olympics. Sapporo's population was listed as 1,241,000 in 1975, but it has grown since then and is Japan's seventh largest city.

Hokkaido is cold during the winter, with temperatures averaging minus five degrees centigrade during January and February. The heavy annual snowfall, along with the mountainous terrain, make it very attractive for skiing, and one resort, Furano, is now a regular stop on the international World Cup Ski Tour.

While the police in Tokyo and the southern areas of Japan have been described by Western scholars, Hokkaido's police force has never been studied in any depth. Furthermore, given the preeminent position of the Tokyo Metropolitan Police Department, I decided that a study of a regional police force would lend some balance to my research. The Tokyo Metropolitan Police Department is at the cutting edge of new developments in policing and has been since the Meiji era, but I also wanted to see a typical Japanese police force.

Policing Hokkaido

While the Hokkaido Prefectural Police is referred to formally as a "Communications Division," in fact, along with the Tokyo Metropolitan Police Department (see Fig. 2), it functions like the seven other regional police forces.

My contacts with Hokkaido Prefectural Police began during the early part of 1981, when I started planning sessions with the vice chiefs of the Patrol and Crime Prevention Divisions. I had to become acquainted with a structure that is somewhat different from that of the Tokyo M.P.D. The organizational chart of Hokkaido Prefectural Police provides an outline of the major departments and lists some of their functions (see Fig. 3). "Security" and "foreign affairs" are euphemisms for intelligence-gathering. Interestingly, the *kidōtai*, or riot police, are placed in the same section. The Crime Prevention Division occupies a position parallel to other divisions such as patrol and traffic. This is characteristic of other prefectural police agencies as well, and reflects the importance the Japanese attach to this function.

The principle concern of the Hokkaido police, however, became apparent in one of my early discussions with the vice chief of the Patrol Division, who remarked that, "Patrolmen are the face of the police—they're always interacting with citizens." Because of the rural nature of the territory, there are 506 *chūzaisho*, as opposed to only 291 *kōban*, in Hokkaido. The problems of police–community relations and defining the proper role of the police officer are particularly crucial to the functioning of these residential *chūzaisho*, and the administration is conscious of the fact that it is the behavior of the men who staff these *chūzaisho* that is viewed as the real nature of the police by citizens.

While there might be some debate on this point, I believe the same is true of American police. Despite a number of ingenious efforts, many United States programs advertised as police–community relations have been superficial public relations approaches. Therefore, the true relationship of police and community in the United States has been very much a function of the day-to-day relationships of patrol police and citizens. None of this is meant to suggest that creative strategies and programs of police departments might not yield major dividends for police–community relations, but just that most programs designated as "police–community relations" to date have been rather thin.

An ideal relationship between a patrol officer and the citizens he serves is not easily achieved. As the vice chief of the Crime Prevention Division observed, there are problems both in becoming too friendly and in remaining too distant. In the view of this veteran officer, "One must stand at the neutral point." He explained that a *kōban* or *chūzaisho* officer cannot mingle freely in the neighborhood. If an officer is friendly with one person, others may suspect him of favoritism. Moreover, administrators are concerned that close friendships between police and citizens render the officers vulnerable to corruption. Hence, officers are rotated every few years to prevent such ties from developing.

Since the system was first introduced, the *chūzaisho* officer (or *chūzai-san*, as he is called) has traditionally been able to develop closer relationships with the people in his district than his urban counterpart in the *kōban*. While administrators may hope that the *chūzai-san* will concentrate on being vigilant, the actual circumstances of the social setting—usually a small village community—encourage a friendly, helpful attitude on the part of the officer, rather than an official, formal one. Usually, he has the luxury of being able to spend more time in visits to households than does the *kōban* officer. The isolation of some rural outposts means that the *chūzai-san* does not have the company of fellow officers on a regular basis and thus must turn to family and neighbors for companionship. People in rural areas are generally more interdependent in their relationships.

In contrast, the dormitory-style living of a considerable number of police in the cities, particularly young, single officers, contributes

Figure 3

Organizational Chart of Hokkaido Prefectural Police
As of 1979

Prime Minister	National Public Safety Commission	- - - - -

Hokkaido Public
Safety Commission - - - - - -

(DIVISIONS)

General Affairs	Police Administrative	Criminal Investigation	Crime Prevention	Patrol

(SECTIONS)

General Affairs	Police Administrative	Criminal Affairs	Crime Prevention	Patrol
Public Rel.	Education	1st–4th Criminal Investigation	Juvenile	Radio Directive
Finance	Welfare	Criminal Identification	Public Safety	Mobile Patrol Unit
Equipment	Complaint & Inspection	Mobile Investigation Unit	Environmental Affairs	
		Scientific Crime Laboratory		Highway Patrol Unit / Expresswa Patrol Un

Each Area Hqs. has own Regional Public Safety Commission.

Sapporo Area Headquarters	Hakodate Area Headquarters	Asahikawa Area Headquarters
NB. Prefectural Hqs. includes the above	General Affairs Section	(Same as the left but excluding the Foreign Affairs Section)
	Finance	
	Police Administrative	
	Complaint & Inspection	
	Criminal Investigation	
	Criminal Identification	
	Crime Prevention	
	Patrol	
	Traffic	
	Highway Patrol Unit	
	Police Guard	
	Foreign Affairs	
28 Police Stations	9 Police Stations	12 Police Stations
348 Police Boxes	98 Police Boxes	151 Police Boxes
161 *Kōban*	31 *Kōban*	40 *Kōban*
187 *Chūzaisho*	69 *Chūzaisho*	111 *Chūzaisho*

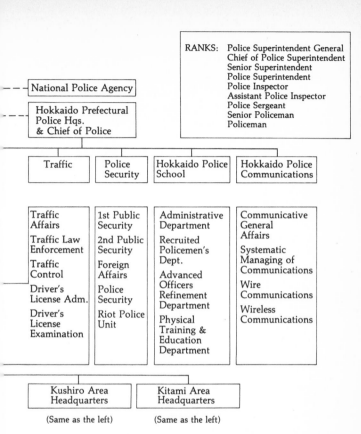

National Police Agency				RANKS:	Police Superintendent General

RANKS:
Police Superintendent General
Chief of Police Superintendent
Senior Superintendent
Police Superintendent
Police Inspector
Assistant Police Inspector
Police Sergeant
Senior Policeman
Policeman

National Police Agency

Hokkaido Prefectural Police Hqs. & Chief of Police

Traffic	Police Security	Hokkaido Police School	Hokkaido Police Communications
Traffic Affairs	1st Public Security	Administrative Department	Communicative General Affairs
Traffic Law Enforcement	2nd Public Security	Recruited Policemen's Dept.	Systematic Managing of Communications
Traffic Control	Foreign Affairs	Advanced Officers Refinement Department	Wire Communications
Driver's License Adm.	Police Security	Physical Training & Education Department	Wireless Communications
Driver's License Examination	Riot Police Unit		

Kushiro Area Headquarters	Kitami Area Headquarters
(Same as the left)	(Same as the left)

10 Police Stations	7 Police Stations
125 Police Boxes	73 Police Boxes
43 *Kōban*	16 *Kōban*
82 *Chūzaisho*	57 *Chūzaisho*

to a sense of community and cohesiveness among officers. Critics charge that it also creates a certain insularity among police and a bit of the "we" and "they" feeling so prevalent between American police and citizens. For example, a probation officer noted that the complex for police in Ebetsu (a city in Hokkaido), which houses around 120 police officers and their families, is referred to as being of the *kidōtai* by nearby residents. *Kidōtai* is the word for the sometimes fearsome riot control police, and applying it to this housing area reflects the subtle hostility and apprehension felt by the citizens. Another person informed me that children of police officers are sometimes treated differently by their classmates in school; other youngsters feel they cannot "fight" with sons and daughters of policemen. In cities, these disadvantages seem to be outweighed by the advantage of having the police together in their own housing complex, ready for mobilization in case of an emergency. In much of Hokkaido, where the force is represented by one man in a residential *chūzaisho*, police–community relations, for better or worse, are much more personal.

When a new officer arrives at a police box, whether it is residential or non-residential, he must try to get to know the people in his area. Ideally he would get to know all of the people in his jurisdiction, but he is most concerned about the persons he must interview as part of the residential survey. The task is made more difficult if he is officious. New recruits among both American and Japanese police tend to accentuate the "professional" role; but in Japan, the general attitude is as important as the actual performance. For instance, if an officer rigorously enforces traffic regulations, he will not be approached by citizens as frequently with tips on criminal offenses.

The head of the Miyuki *kōban* in Sapporo estimated that through the routine family visits and confidential files kept at police boxes, the officers know approximately ninety percent of the residents in terms of basic information but are only able to match the names and faces of neighboring residents.

The Chūzai-san

From the early days of policing, the *chūzai-san* has occupied an honored place in the community and, along with the village head-man and school principal, has been considered one of the top-ranking town officials (e.g., see R. P. Dore, *Shinohata: A Portrait of a Japanese Village*, 1978), and, residing in a police box with his wife and family, is naturally integrated into the life of the community. Thus, while administrators may set a policy that urges a "neutral" stance, the nature of rural life encourages close ties between an officer and his community.

Practices such as the officer leaving behind his name card (*meishi*) when he visits a home that he finds unlocked and with no one at home help to cement ties. The *meishi* has the officer's name on one side, and frequently he writes a note on the other. Ever alert to his crime prevention role, he might comment on something that indicated the house was empty: "The many milk bottles that have accumulated during your absence are an invitation to criminals. Therefore you should suspend the milk delivery when you are away." Since police behavior in Japan reflects a moral norm as much as a legal one, this type of note with its paternalistic tone is acceptable. Most Americans would regard such a note as over-ly intrusive.

Police in Japan appear to use print media to a much greater ex-tent than American police. Three-quarters of *chūzaisho* and *kō-ban* publish their own short articles and notices in local newspapers; circulars are also distributed. Contents vary from reports on crimes and accidents to specific crime prevention measures, explanations of laws, citizens' opinions, and children's activities. Events of in-terest to the community and profiles of citizens who perform outstanding services are often included. Police–community rela-tions are also enhanced by telephone lines called "*Jūmin* Corner" (*jūmin* means "resident"), which have been established in a number of prefectures to allow people to call in with various problems. This service will be described in more detail later.

Attitudes of rural citizens toward the police are different from those of their urban counterparts. One officer assigned to Konbu *chūzaisho* noted that when he had worked at the busiest police station in Sapporo, engaged in traffic investigation, people gave only necessary, minimum information. In his new rural outpost, hundreds of miles from Sapporo, people volunteered information and at times sought him out for conversation. One elderly man came regularly to the *chūzaisho* to talk. One day he came at around 7 A.M. and the officer invited him in for breakfast. Due to the heavy annual snowfall in this mountainous area, the officer also occasionally helped motorists shovel out. While he actively encouraged residents to bring their problems to him, because of his brief tenure of just ten months, people still preferred to seek out the town assemblyman. The Konbu *chūzaisho* is responsible for more than 114.3 square kilometers (43 square miles), but there are just 450 houses and commercial enterprises in that large area. As with many one-man rural *chūzaisho*, a mini-patrol car is provided. Most of this officer's time was spent in routine family visits and an occasional traffic investigation. He informed me that there were no husband–wife domestic fights brought to his attention during his ten months at this location.

A visit to the two-man Niseko *chūzaisho* offered only slight variations of the *chūzai-san*'s role. This police box is located in the center of a village of 4,595 people. Because the nearby hot springs and mountain trails attract tourists in the summer and skiers in the winter, the principal duty of Niseko police is giving directions. The police estimate that forty-five percent of their time is spent with directions, twenty percent with traffic accidents, and just ten percent with crimes, with the other twenty-five percent spent on administrative matters or other duties. Crimes are for the most part petty theft. There was one report a few months prior to my visit of an altercation between six drunken construction workers and two highway patrol officers. The problem occurred when the car the workers were riding in was stopped at midnight because it was weaving all over the road. The occupants became incensed and started punching the police. Another incident had occurred the previous July: several workers became involved in a street fight during a Niseko festival, probably as a result of drinking. These were among the few incidents of violence that police could recall during the previous year.

The Kuchan region encompasses five towns and two villages and has a population of around 38,000. Fifty police officers and six civilians are assigned to this station area, which includes one *kōban* and twelve *chūzaisho*. For the entire region covered by the Kuchan station there had been just two homicides in the previous ten-year period. In one case, a young man murdered a high school classmate who had rebuffed his sexual advances. In the other case, a bar hostess had been murdered by a *yakuza* (gangster). There were an estimated twelve or thirteen such gangsters engaging in gambling and narcotics-trafficking in Kuchan. The head of this local group was reputed to be a "lieutenant" to the chief of a larger group in Otaru.

In 1979, there were approximately 9,000 residential police boxes in Japan, a reduction from the 10,239 that existed just five years earlier. As Japan has become more urbanized, officials have moved to replace *chūzaisho* with *kōban*. The geographical area covered by a *chūzaisho* jurisdiction is usually almost four times greater than that of a *kōban*. For example, the largest jurisdiction in Hokkaido covers almost half the area of Osaka Prefecture. In addition to this unwieldy size, *chūzaisho* service presents problems for the officers. While hours are 8:30 A.M. to 5:30 P.M., Monday through Friday, and 8:30 A.M. to 12:30 P.M. on Saturday, many requests are made "after hours." The National Police Agency guidelines indicate that residential police officers should have Sundays off. Coverage is provided by reassigning other personnel or, in case of an emergency, a phone is available on Sunday at the frequently vacant police box. Nevertheless, it is not uncommon to hear *chūzaisho* police complain about the feeling of being "always on duty." Families of officers also suffer from the disruptions, and the wives of *chūzai-san*, in fact, receive a nominal wage for assisting their husbands. This duty seems to require a certain type of officer, with a particularly supportive family. Often, the *chūzai-san* I met came from rural backgrounds and thus had less difficulty with the adjustment. One example of a man who thoroughly enjoyed his work follows.

Profile of a Chūzai-san

This particular man was one of the most delightful police officers I met during my stay in Japan. He was a *chūzaisho* officer working in an outlying area covered by the Tokyo Metropolitan Police Department. I spent several days at his police box observing his daily routine and interactions with citizens. I was surprised to find that there are residential police boxes under the M.P.D.'s jurisdiction until I learned how large and diversified the Tokyo metropolitan area is. This man—Officer Saitō let us call him— was thirty-seven years old, married, and had three daughters. His rank was sergeant. He had always sought a residential police box assignment. Born and raised in an agricultural community far to the south of Tokyo, he had considered taking over his parents' farm but had decided against it. "These days," he said, "the oldest son is not automatically expected to take over the farm. Rather, the son who likes the work will take it over." He traced his early interest in police work to the "little kindnesses" he had observed the local officer offering to neighbors in his community. He had hoped to avoid working in a large city, but it proved to be his only access to police work. After completing high school, he had been assigned to Nakano for the required one year of police training. Later, he took evening courses at his own expense at Nippon University, an institution based in Tokyo with over a hundred thousand students. Eventually, he received his degree. He had been a policeman for seventeen years and had worked in a variety of other police assignments, including traffic control, and his last assignment before receiving this posting had been in a jail working with pre-sentence detainees. Police administrators tend to agree that married, slightly older officers like Saitō are the best choice for *chūzaisho* assignments, but, according to one official in Chiba Prefecture, they are increasingly difficult to find.

Saitō was friendly and outgoing and appeared to enjoy thoroughly the most trivial, mundane encounters with citizens. He went out of his way to make such meetings agreeable. His police box was gaily decorated with flowers, and a colorful bird chattered in a cage near the window. This *chūzaisho* is located in a park, across the street from a cemetery and with a number of cherry trees nearby. It was the first *chūzaisho* I visited, and the setting was so idyllic that I found myself wondering at the time whether or not it had been "spruced up" for my benefit. Later, after visiting other flower-bedecked *chūzaisho*, my skepticism vanished.

Saitō said he found his job very enjoyable because it allowed him to get to know people and that, in his opinion, was the most important part of a *chūzai-san's* job. This seemed evident when he conducted the residential survey, visiting neighborhood homes, shopkeepers, and the residence of a Buddhist priest. His wife was cooperative and helped by answering the phone and occasionally assisting with a drunk. He noted, "When drunks are talking to women, they are less aggressive."

In discussing police work, he remarked that most officers are very committed, that morale is high, and that while some people, like his brother, feel that the police take their duties too seriously, he disagreed. He added that the discipline of police work creates a sense of pride in many officers.

A number of officers I interviewed provided thoughtful answers to my questions. For example, in response to the question, "How much does society or one's life circumstances versus one's own sense of responsibility contribute to criminal activity?" Saitō answered, "They both do, although it is difficult to separate the individual's control over his own behavior from society's impact upon him. In the case of a young person who gets involved with a particular group, he may be under pressure to commit a delinquent act. However, I believe the person must try to resist the pressure of the group and act with responsibility." Then, somewhat as an afterthought, he said, "It's my job to improve the environment."

He demonstrated compassion toward offenders when I asked, "Once arrested for a serious crime like rape, murder, or robbery, how should criminals be treated by the authorities (i.e., courts and prisons)?" He answered, "They may be disturbed and they may need to be handled with care—otherwise they will feel isolated if put into prison. Everybody has the potential of committing a crime, and the authorities should make sure that a person who comes out of prison is able to live independently." It is uncommon to hear American police express concern for the conditions in prison and often they express contempt for offenders. Saitō's compassion was tempered with realism, however, when I asked specifically about the rehabilitation potential of adult offenders. He viewed youthful offenders as having a good potential for living a crime-free life if they are provided with education and/or job training, but he acknowledged that with serious offenders, many returned to crime. "When one commits a crime, it reflects on the rest," he observed, referring to the interdependence and mutual responsibility felt by Japanese family members, coworkers, and friends.

While enjoying the social interaction of his job, Saitō was also required to make more official observations at times. For example, he was participating in an investigation of radical students, who, though fewer in number and generally less active than during the late sixties, are still considered dangerous, as well as difficult to locate and arrest. Though he claimed he did not enjoy doing it, he said that for this kind of work it was necessary to learn what one could, even during the friendly routine family visits.

Saitō's jurisdiction included 467 households and businesses in which 1,300 persons lived and worked. His muscular frame reminded one of a football fullback, and, combined with his husky voice, it belied his friendly attitude toward local residents. He hailed almost everyone who walked past his police box. Like a number of officers I met, he enjoyed giving judo lessons to neighborhood children, in this case a class of seventeen youngsters. Saitō sees judo as an activity that discourages juvenile delinquency and "builds character." He could not resist a slight parenthetical admonishment to parents who were "too careful about their children." He maintained that children should learn "fighting spirit." Like many sports enthusiasts, he felt that the benefits of physical conditioning flowed into other areas. Some mothers had voiced concern that the judo training would affect the study habits of their children, a subject that obsesses Japanese parents, but he had allayed their fears. In his eyes, judo served as a vehicle for developing better relationships not only with the children he taught but with their parents as well.

Earlier in his career with the M.P.D., he had been frustrated with his traffic assignment, and in contrast the *chūzaisho* allowed him a much greater variety of tasks that he enjoyed. Other *chū-*

zai-san who enjoyed the work voiced similar sentiments. This sense of job fulfillment was so deeply felt by him that if promotion meant reassignment he preferred to stay at his rank of sergeant and remain at this location.

It would be misleading to fail to point out that there are police officers in the United States who function much like the *chūzai-san*. As in Japan, these officers are found in small towns and rural areas.

One such American was described by L. Rout in an article for *The Wall Street Journal*. He is "Virgil," the sheriff of Grant County, South Dakota. During his thirty years as sheriff, he fired his gun just once—straight up into the sky. He patrols a sprawling jurisdiction of over 750 square miles, and like his rural counterpart in Japan, he spent most of his time counseling and visiting people. The service aspect of his job predominated in his territory of 9,000 inhabitants. While he served summonses, took care of prisoners, and collected taxes, his personal relationships were such that one county resident remarked, "Virgil is God around here; you have a problem about anything, you call Virgil."[1]

Visits to Other Chūzaisho

Unlike the situation with the Tokyo Metropolitan Police Department, in which officers are frequently drawn from outside the M.P.D.'s jurisdiction, the Hokkaido Prefectural Police select most of their men from the island of Hokkaido. It is also not uncommon to hear that an officer's father or another relative was a policeman.

The Ishikari *chūzaisho* took one hour to reach by driving north from Sapporo in a blinding snowstorm. The police box is just 200 meters from the Sea of Japan. It is staffed by one officer and serves the village of Ishikari, which has 3,000 inhabitants. Like his counterpart in Konbu, this officer was required to spend time during the winter clearing snow away from the police box. The daily routine usually consisted of processing paperwork—perhaps including a report on a traffic accident—for an hour or so in the morning. This *chūzai-san* estimated that he would have approximately forty-five accidents to report on during any given year, fifteen of which might involve personal injury. After completing any snow clearing or report writing that was required, he would go out on patrol, usually on foot, but occasionally in his mini-patrol car. After lunch, for approximately two hours, he would make routine visits to residences and to the handful of commercial establishments in this small town. Late in the afternoon, he would work on traffic control, winding up his day with some paperwork. Officially, he would stop work at 6 P.M. Like other *chūzai-san*, he was not infrequently called after he had closed the front office area of the building. He estimated that every two or three days he would receive a call concerning a traffic accident or perhaps one about a drunk who was sleeping in the street. Occasionally, he was called upon after hours to give directions.

Generally, there was little criminal activity for the sergeant to be concerned with in Ishikari. For example, in the previous year, sixteen thefts were reported, including four house burglaries and two automobile thefts. There were three reported instances of theft from unlocked motor vehicles. One homicide had occurred, but this was considered extremely unusual; an emotionally disturbed man who had just come to town killed his younger brother with a knife. An additional dozen or so incidents, including fights and a person who refused to pay a bill in a restaurant, were all there was to report for the previous year.

This *chūzai-san* seemed to strive for the middle ground in relationships with citizens. Choosing not to work hard at fostering close relations with local citizens, he nevertheless would occasionally go drinking with some of them. However, he commented that he was always mindful of the fact that he might have to turn around and "lecture" one of them for speeding.

Like other officers, he viewed the recent decade as a period when people had become more concerned about expressing their individuality and less interested in "serving others." He was concerned that decreasing cooperation among community residents did not augur well for the future of crime control.

Juvenile delinquency in this rural community took the form of group theft, running away from home, and sexual promiscuity. He cited a recent case of a high school girl who had frequently arranged nighttime visits by her boyfriend to her room in her parents' home. According to the sergeant, this situation would not have arisen ten years earlier, and could be attributed to the increased tendency for parents to give their children their own rooms. In an attempt to keep abreast of the juvenile situation, he would meet with schoolteachers and administrators to discuss problem students. While this officer was willing to counsel juveniles or adults with problems at the police box, he acknowledged that some felt a reluctance to come to him for assistance. Along with the fear of becoming the subject of rumors, he said that most people wished to "solve their own problems."

Contacts with *chūzai-san* and observations at other residential police boxes provided information that generally conformed with the examples sketched above. A veteran of eight years at one *chūzaisho* in the Tokyo area complained at length about the system of evaluation. It is inherently unfair, he claimed, because it is based on brief, intermittent visits by supervisors. In addition, there is no "feed-back" for the officer from these evaluations. The officer maintained that these feelings are shared by other *chūzai-san*.

Observations of police boxes in Sapporo, such as at the Susukino and Miyuki *kōban*, yielded information similar to that which I had gathered earlier in Tokyo. The Susukino police box was located in the heart of a brightly lit entertainment district. As a consequence, police were concerned about controlling the activity of overly aggressive pimps. Susukino is quite famous in Japan as a prostitution quarter, and there are more than 3,500 pubs, cabarets, and restaurants compressed into this small district, as well as some eighty-five Turkish baths that also offer sex to their customers. As in other districts of this kind in Japan, *yakuza* (gangsters) have made inroads into the nightclub and cabaret businesses. In the previous year, a "turf" battle had erupted between a gang from Honshu and a local Hokkaido group with the outsiders being rebuffed. Once again, despite this huge amount of nighttime activity and the element of organized crime, there were just two incidents involving firearms. In one case, a *yakuza* had accidentally fired a weapon, while in another a member of the same group had been charged with the illegal possession of a firearm.

NOTES
1. L. Rout, "Rural Justice: Old-Fashioned Sheriff of Grant Country, South Dakota, Doubles As a Friend," *The Wall Street Journal*, August 10, 1981, p. 1.

Chapter 5

THE INVESTIGATION OF CRIME

The amount of crime in Japan, as in the United States, is only partly a function of the efficiency and quality of the justice system. The basic nature of the society must also be considered. The role of the justice system, however, is perhaps larger in Japan. In many ways, although it is a cliché, "crime does not pay" for the Japanese. The chances of a criminal being caught are greater than in the United States, due partly to the simple fact that Japan is an island only slightly larger than California. A very important additional factor in Japan is that there is no plea bargaining, the negotiating between lawyers and judges that frequently reduces the seriousness of the charge.

Clearance rates, a favorite topic of justice officials in both countries, are remarkably different in Japan and the United States. Generally, the U.S. Department of Justice considers a crime cleared "when a law enforcement agency has identified the offender, has sufficient evidence to charge him and actually takes him into custody."[1] The *Uniform Crime Reports* (U.S. Department of Justice, 1980) of the F.B.I. indicated that for violent crime (murder, rape, robbery, and aggravated assault) in 1979, an average of just 51.2 percent of all crimes were cleared. Contrast that figure with 92 percent for violent crime cleared by Japanese police (National Police Agency, 1980). Data for larceny is equally impressive: 19 percent in the United States and 54.7 percent in Japan. Larceny generally covers pickpockets, shoplifters, purse-snatchers, bicycle thieves, etc., that is, crimes where no use of force, violence, or fraud occurs. Furthermore, there was a 1.1 percent increase in clearance rates for all crimes in Japan from 1978 to 1979. For the same period, a decline of 1 percent was recorded in the United States.

Complementing the police efficiency reflected in the high clearance rates are strong psychological pressures within the tightly woven, competitive Japanese society for citizens to conform and obey the law. Japanese who commit crimes and who come to the attention of justice officials generally feel a deep sense of shame. Family members and relatives feel an obligation to deter illegal acts. If an individual is arrested, his family feels responsible— much like the embarrassment and shame the individual himself may feel. Though families in the United States may have similar feelings, they are much more pronounced among the Japanese. Nor is this sense of shared shame confined to families of offenders. For example, in 1980 a police officer raped a woman and the chief of his police station felt obligated to resign. (It should be noted that it is extremely rare for a police officer to be convicted of assaulting a citizen.) This action was taken despite the fact that the police station chief was in no way directly responsible for the offender; he did not even directly supervise the officer. However, in Japan, it is expected that the person in charge assume a significant share of the responsibility.

In the United States, there appears to be a continuing erosion of respect for authority and for life itself. In 1981, *The New York Times* conducted an extensive interview with New York City's highly respected police commissioner at that time, Robert J. McGuire, who commented:

> I am concerned about the general lack of respect for and adherence to law in this city in a quality of life sense. There is a sense that young people, specifically young people, have actually no respect for other people's property. That they vandalize parks, they vandalize anything they can get their hands on. I think there has to be a recognition that there has been a tremendous deterioration of compliance with law in our society. And I'm not a social scientist. But it seems clear to

me and other police administrators that you have many, many people today willing to commit crimes. Right now you have a message out that more often than not crime pays.[2]

He continued about the police in New York City:

Historically, they were a symbol of authority. They didn't have to assert themselves. People were afraid of them. Kids were afraid of them. That's no longer true today. Criminals shoot at them, and kids show them absolutely total disrespect.[3]

In short, criminals are rewarded far more often than they are punished for their illegal acts. Cultural restraints are weaker than in Japan, and the ease with which juvenile and adult offenders alike can commit crimes reinforces their behavior.

Another factor in the sharply higher United States crime rate seems to be the weakened family structure, reflected in the higher frequency of broken families and divorce. American families no longer provide young people with fixed standards of right and wrong behavior to the same degree as Japanese families. In Japan there were just 1.14 divorces per 1,000 population in 1978, while in the United States the rate was 5.2 per 1,000 population (U.S. Bureau of the Census, 1980). Divorce has been on the rise in Japan in recent years but not at the accelerated American rate, as the figures in Table 2 indicate. Of course, it must be remembered that the population of the United States was around 220 million in 1979 as opposed to Japan's 115 million.

Table 2
Total Divorces

	Japan	United States
1963	70,000	428,000
1972	108,000	845,000
1978	132,000	1,130,000
1979	142,000	1,170,000

Many criminal acts in the United States are committed due to circumstances of social and economic deprivation that do not exist in Japan, where middle-class affluence is widespread. Racism continues to flourish in the United States, and it is exceedingly difficult for many minorities raised in neighborhoods such as the South Bronx and Bedford-Stuyvesant to improve their standard of living. Thus, from their perspective, they have something to gain and little to lose by risking a criminal act.

The beginning of most criminal investigations is, of course, the citizen's report that a crime has occurred. The Japanese report crime, as noted previously, at a rate that comes closer to the actual incidence than Americans do. Therefore, the huge discrepancy in reported crimes between Japan and America is probably even larger for the actual occurrence of crime.

Both countries now conduct direct household "victimization" surveys. Japan's National Police Agency, in a survey of victimization conducted in 1969, compared responses from a random sample of 15,000 households reflecting various income levels and found that the number of unreported crimes was 1.005 times the number of reported offenses. A similar survey in 1972 by the same agency found the rate for the Tokyo metropolitan area to be 0.69 (National Statement of Japan, 1980).

In the United States, the National Crime Survey, conducted every six months by the Bureau of Justice Statistics, interviews nearly 132,000 members of 60,000 households throughout America (U.S. Department of Justice, 1981). In a 1977 publication, the U.S. Department of Justice stated that the unreported rate of "index" crimes (homicide, rape, robbery, aggravated assault, burglary, larceny, and auto theft) was more than twice the rate of reported crime listed in the F.B.I.'s *Uniform Crime Reports*. Figures published later (U.S. Department of Justice, 1980) confirmed that for the years 1978 and 1979, the above-mentioned crimes of "violence" continued at twice the rate of reported crime. For simple assault, Americans reported a mere 37.4 percent to the police for 1979, while for rape 55.5 percent (up 5.5 percent over the previous year) was reported during the same year. Fifty-one percent of aggravated assaults were reported to United States authorities during 1979.

There were approximately four times as many personal and household larcenies as the number reported during 1979 (U.S. Department of Justice, 1980). One encouraging sign for Americans has been the drop of 4 percent in overall crime for 1982, and a decline of 5 percent for the first six months of 1983, as reported by the F.B.I.

Violence

While less violence exists in Japan than in the United States, recent instances of violent crime have shocked the Japanese people. Particularly disturbing is the increase in "senseless" crimes, those that are perpetrated on strangers without any apparent motive. During my stay in Japan, there was a noticeable rise in newspaper reports of such crimes, which often resulted in the victim's death. In one case, an apparently emotionally disturbed man tossed a firebomb into a Tokyo bus, killing several people. Another case involved a middle-aged man who stabbed two women and two children to death on a Tokyo street, then took another woman hostage and held her at a nearby restaurant. While this sort of random crime is, unfortunately, not uncommon in the United States, it has only recently become a problem in Japan.

It is unclear as yet whether these crimes, called *tōrima*, or "passing devil," attacks, will establish themselves as a trend. They are generally attributed to the mental instability of the accused, often brought on by the extraordinary pressures of the highly organized and competitive Japanese society. The outbursts can occasionally be traced to some particular failure or disgrace, such as being unable to pass the entrance examination to a university. But such explanations are little comfort to the police, who are beginning to experience the same bewilderment familiar to their American counterparts in the face of such meaningless, patternless, and thus unpreventable crime.

Another type of violent crime was noted by *The Japan Times* (October 17, 1980) during the year of my research. A series of forty-seven "knock down" cases were reported to the police from April 1980 through mid-October of the same year. Around ¥1,544,000 (approximately $7,000) was stolen from the victims.

Most of those robbed were drunks over fifty who were knocked down in alleys near entertainment centers or railway stations between 9 P.M. and midnight. The robbers operated in groups of two to four and appeared to be between twenty-five and thirty years of age, according to reports given to the Tokyo Metropolitan Police Department. Though these muggings pale when compared to those in New York City or Chicago for a similar period, they represent an alarming increase in violence from the Japanese point of view.

However, notwithstanding this recent rash of crimes, the overall rate of felonious crime has remained at a stable, low level over the past decade. Attempting to understand why violent crime for the most part is so well controlled in Japan leads inevitably back to the discussion of Japanese society, with its emphasis on group values and conformity. Japanese values and customs are the key to this phenomenon.

On two different occasions, I asked a group of social scientists at the National Police Agency's National Research Institute of Police Science for their views on the role of violence and aggression in Japan. Haruo Nishimura, a psychologist, opened the discussion by noting that, "Aggressive people are not well received here." He added, "We do not like to express everything directly." Verbal communication is typically more indirect and polite in Japan with fewer direct confrontations. While some Japanese concede that the "frankness" of Westerners is appealing, they point out that it is achieved at the price of rudeness and hurt feelings. The emphasis in Japan is placed on getting along and promoting interpersonal harmony with as few conflicts as possible. While Americans, upon their arrival in Japan, are often frustrated initially by the lack of candor they perceive in their relationships with Japanese, eventually many come to appreciate the subtlety and nuances of Japanese social relations.

The following points were suggested by the above-mentioned group at the National Research Institute of Police Science—a group that, in addition to Haruo Nishimura, included Yoshiaki Takahashi, Shingo Suzuki, and Kanehiro Hoshino. These statements might be described as widely shared views held by the Japanese about their society:

—The low level of violence is significantly related to the socialization process. At a very early age, parents teach their children that aggression will not be tolerated.

—Teachers exert strong controls on the expression of violence and/or aggression. Two- or three-day suspensions from classes are not unusual if a child acts up even in a minor way.

—The homogeneous nature of Japanese society, with less than one percent of the population being non-Japanese, contributes to a greater degree of empathy for one another.

—There are relatively few broken families in Japan and the divorce rate is generally low, despite a slight increase in recent years. As noted earlier, for 1978 there were just 1.14 divorces (per 1,000 population) in Japan.

—The environment is less stressful in Japan according to these social scientists, several of whom had studied at the University of Chicago or at Harvard. While life is fast-paced, particularly in the major cities, there are environmental supports that help to cushion the consequences of modern urban life. These include such things as the job security offered by the lifetime employment system of many companies and the emphasis on group life in which fellow workers, students, or neighbors offer emotional and social support to each other.

—Many women work in the home; their adaptation to the roles of homemaker and wife has helped to ease the tensions inherent in Japan's crowded, industrialized society. While women are increasingly accepting full-time jobs outside of the home, with higher-salaried jobs becoming available, most still aspire to be housewives. (Admittedly, this opinion was offered by a group of male social scientists. To what extent women scholars or women in general would agree with this assertion is open to question.)

—Japanese society offers many forms of recreation and leisure activity. It is common for groups of workers to go off together to a resort for a few days of fun and recreation, enjoying the camaraderie that they prize. Workers frequently drink saké together or play popular games like mah-jongg or *pachinko* after work. (Another outlet is provided by the attention and caresses of Japanese hostesses in nightclubs and cabarets.)

This list was not, of course, intended as a comprehensive statement of the factors contributing to the lack of violence in Japan. Nonetheless, I think it provides a good framework for understanding this remarkable phenomenon.

There is, unfortunately, no way for an outsider (nor for that matter, I suspect, an insider) to tell whether the police institutions are a cause or an effect of this social system. Do the powerful and respected police draw that power from this willingness to be obedient and cooperative, or does the obedience come from the constant pressure from powerful authorities, first in the family and then in society at large? The answer, of course, is obscured in the national history and psychology, but it is doubtful that either history or psychology will be of much help in uncovering it. Obedience and authority are almost a single phenomenon in Japan. I am not hoping here to solve that puzzle, but to describe an aspect of it. We have looked at the grass roots level of policing—the cop on the beat, or in this case in the *kōban* or *chūzaisho*. I would now like to look at the role of another authority figure who is at a different place in the hierarchy but has perhaps equally far-reaching power to promote law and order, namely, the public prosecutor.

The Role of the Public Prosecutor

The grass roots investigation of crime, including violent crime, is for the most part conducted by police officers, but prosecutors play a major supervisory and policy-making role. They occupy a powerful position with broad-ranging authority to pursue as well as suspend prosecution of cases. Public Prosecutor Shikita, in a Japan Society seminar held in New York in 1980, described prosecutors as having a quasi-judicial function:

> Each prosecutor is authorized to decide on the appropriate scope of investigation, to decide whether to prosecute at all and, if so, on what charges and, finally, to request the imposition of sentence as he feels appropriate. Decisions are to be based only on the interplay of the individual prosecutor's

conscience with the "substantive truth" as he discovers it. Thus, he is not merely an assistant to the agency head but is vested with independent powers. In this sense, a prosecutor's decision-making process is similar to that of a judge.[4]

Clifford expands on this independence of judgment and the discretionary power of the prosecutor:

> However nobly impartial the courts in the West might be, the Japanese, like so many of the Chinese thinkers, preferred to take the blindfold off the symbol of justice and to take a closer look at the scales they were balancing. Discretion was necessary to them to take account of the special circumstances of each crime and to apply the law only when necessary. If a *penalty* could be mitigated by circumstances, so could a charge. Here again was the familiar particularism of Japanese thinking being opposed to the universalism of the West. For the West, justice is a matter of principle. The Japanese accept that, but only with the proviso that the principle needs to be adjusted to take account of special circumstances. Thus a public prosecutor in Japan may suspend prosecution at his own discretion, even if the evidence is sufficient to ensure a conviction, if he believes it to be in the best interest of society and the offender.[5]

In discussions of the history of the role of the prosecutor in Japan, one frequently reads accounts of the European origins of the system, not unlike the case of the police discussed earlier. In this connection, during the early Meiji period samurai visited France, Germany, and other European countries to study their legal systems. The resulting institution, known as the "procurator" in Japan, had wide discretionary powers to prosecute or not to prosecute certain cases. Nagashima (in Von Mehren, ed., 1963) explains, however, that the role of defense counsel was rather limited until the influence of Anglo-American law was felt in the post–Second World War period. H. Tanaka is very critical of both the defense counsels and public prosecutors during the early part of the twentieth century:

In the field of criminal law as well, the Japanese notion of law seems to have been pretty much different from that of the Westerners. Though at the level of theory, we imported, during the Meiji Era, the Western concept of emphasizing the role of criminal law in protecting an individual from the power of the state, much time was needed before this concept took root in our soil. This becomes obvious if we look at the actual working of criminal law. It is notorious how easily the human rights of suspects were neglected before 1945. The blame for this is not to be ascribed solely to the police, but also must be cast upon public procurators and judges for their failure to develop rules and practices to prevent or discourage such unlawful methods of law enforcement. Turning to practicing attorneys, I cannot help having the impression that only a minority of them fought hard for the protection of the rights of suspects, though I can also give a number of names of those who worked for this objective.[6]

The above-mentioned "quasi-judicial" function of present-day prosecutors is a remnant from a period when they actually were part of the judiciary. Tanaka explains that up until 1974, the prosecutor's office was regarded as one of the components of the judiciary (shihō) and that the intertwining of both judicial and prosecutorial functions resulted in a concentration of the powers of the state. This dual authority in the Ministry of Justice also allowed many prosecutors to have political influence far beyond their prescribed function. Many occupied top positions in this agency. Furthermore, it should be remembered throughout this discussion of the investigation of crimes and prosecution of criminals that jury trials, only briefly in existence, were abandoned by 1943, and all criminal trials were handled by judges.

The present-day prosecutor (or procurator) has a substantial amount of power, and in addition he has a broad range of situations and opportunities throughout the judicial process in which to exercise it. Though generally the prosecutor acts in a supervisory role for an investigation initiated by police, there are occasions in which the prosecutor will initiate the investigation himself. He has that authority. Approximately sixty percent of a prosecutor's time is spent on the investigation of cases, including those handled by police.

Conviction rates in Japanese trials have been running at around 99.8 percent in recent years (Fujiwara, 1980), but prosecutors and Ministry of Justice officials are quick to point out that there are sound reasons for this astonishingly high conviction rate and that it does not reflect weak legal defense. Cases where the evidence is doubtful are not prosecuted in Japan. Tsuchiya (1980) presents an interesting statistic to help support this contention. He notes that prosecutors decided not to prosecute 30 percent of the total number of Penal Code offenders referred from the police in 1976.

Of those who are prosecuted, 77 percent were disposed of by "summary procedures," which will be described later in this chapter. Of the offenders who were sentenced to imprisonment, with or without forced labor, 56 percent were given "suspension of the execution of sentence" in 1976. A total of 830,679 offenders were arrested or investigated by the police for Penal Code offenses in 1976, and only 2.7 percent of them, or 22,680 offenders, were sent to prison. Data cited by Public Prosecutor Shikita at the 1980 Japan Society seminar showed similar percentages for 1978; suspension of prosecution was granted in 37 percent of all non-traffic cases. A breakdown noted that 29 percent of extortion cases, 21 percent of arson cases, and 6.5 percent of homicide cases were identified under "suspension of prosecution granted." Thus, Tsuchiya and other Ministry of Justice officials argue that many offenders are diverted from the criminal justice system at various stages.

Another factor influencing both the low crime rate and high conviction rate is that many crimes that are still "on the books" in Western nations, including the United States, are not treated as crimes in Japan. As examples, Tsuchiya offers vagrancy, homosexuality, and public drunkenness, which have never been considered crimes in Japan. Without the worries caused by these prevalent but victimless offenses, law enforcement authorities are freer to pursue what most people would consider more serious crimes.

A. Nagashima explains another aspect of the role of the Japanese prosecutor that might surprise his counterpart in the United States:

Japanese prosecutors actively consider the rehabilitation prospects of offenders as part of their decision to prosecute or not. This factor is also taken into account at the sentencing stage, should the defendant be convicted. Japanese officials frequently use the term "criminological" in discussing this aspect of their work. In describing the evolving role of the prosecutor in the 1960s, Nagashima noted:

> Before the second Code of Criminal Procedure, there was no provision giving procurators a discretionary power of non-prosecution. Nevertheless, it gradually became general usage for the procurator to decline prosecution of less serious crimes. Because the investigation and disposition of the matter were carried out by the procurator in closed chambers, the identity of the offender against whom prosecution was declined was rarely disclosed to the public; consequently, the offender could continue in the community as a good citizen rather than with the stigma of a criminal. This system contributed so much to the rehabilitation and re-entry of the offender into society that it was explicitly approved and extended in the second code. Even an offender who had committed a rather serious crime might be relieved from prosecution if he was a first offender, if the injuries caused by the offense were compensated for, and if there was reasonable ground to believe that he would not commit another offense.[7]

What Nagashima does not mention in this statement, and what critics are quick to point out, is that while it is true that in cases in which prosecutors decline to prosecute, though offenders are not socially stigmatized with a criminal record, they do remain marked men in the eyes of law enforcement authorities. Shikita stressed that criminological considerations were far more important than "utilitarian reasons" in the decision to grant suspension of prosecution. He stated that "the existence of a confession, sincere repentance by the suspect, and the forgiveness of the victim are important factors"[8] in making this decision.

Fujiwara presents interesting data that help to illuminate the use of "suspension of prosecution" in recent years (see Table 3).

Table 3

Rate of Suspension of Prosecution

	1974	1975	1976	1977	1978
All criminal offenses	12.6	11.7	10.0	9.4	9.1 (265,312)
Penal offenses	33.3	32.2	30.6	30.8	27.6 (183,074)
Penal offenses (except traffic offenses)	41.6	38.1	36.4	37.2	36.9 (80,578)
Violation of the Road Traffic Control Law	3.0	2.7	2.5	2.3	2.5 (52,825)
Other special law offenses	36.2	34.5	26.8	28.3	21.0 (29,413)

$$\text{The rate of suspension of prosecution} = \frac{\text{The number of suspected offenders subjected to suspension of prosecution}}{\text{The number of suspected offenders subjected to prosecution} + \text{The number of suspected offenders subjected to suspension of prosecution}} \times 100$$

Source: T. Fujiwara, "Criminal Justice System in Japan (III): Criminal Investigation." Unpublished paper for the United Nations Asia and Far East Institute for the Prevention of Crime and Treatment of Offenders, Tokyo, fall, 1980.

There are individuals who are skeptical and even highly critical of Japanese justice. English journalist D. Kirk, writing for the London *Observer* (February 2, 1981), noted that eighty-six percent of all cases that go to trial include a confession, which, he sarcastically points out, is still the "king of evidence" in Japan. Interestingly, Japanese authorities do not quibble with his statistic, but interpret it somewhat differently.

An example of such an interpretation can be seen in a paper presented by Public Prosecutor Fujiwara during the fall of 1980 to the training class of Asian justice officials at the United Nations Asia and Far East Institute for the Prevention of Crime and Treatment of Offenders. Perhaps partially because of the tradition of confessing among Japanese, Japanese justice officials are proud of this high rate, while to Americans it smacks of heavy-handedness and coercion. Fujiwara cites the following data for 1977:

> Of a total of 80,792 defendants whose cases have been tried by the court of first instance, 69,524 defendants or eighty-six percent made confessions in court in 1977. When we take the number of summary orders into account, the rate of confession at the investigation stage may be more than ninety percent.[9]

But from the other side of the bench, one prominent Japanese private attorney who has defended many clients mentioned that as the suspect increasingly becomes the target of an investigation, authorities can get "harsh." "Unless you confess readily, questioning will be tough. Most guilty people do confess," he indicated. He noted that police methods had been the subject of three types of Supreme Court cases: those involving the "voluntariness of citizens' cooperation in police questioning"; those involving "police abuse itself" (obviously he meant physical abuse); and, finally, those cases involving "civil damages." Along similar lines, one of my police officer friends who worked as a sergeant in Tokyo, in response to my question about why suspects confess so readily, commented that, "It is no use to protest against power."

Kirk comments that the high conviction rate (he cited 99.7 percent) is due not only to the thoroughness and professionalism of police and prosecutorial authorities but to a "complex array of laws" that gives the prosecutor every advantage. As an example, he cited the fact that judges can review written evidence instead of listening to witnesses who sometimes go back on what they say. This, of course, is a departure from justice in Great Britain and the United States, where witnesses must be present in most cases to answer questions in court. In an interview with Kirk, Akio Harada, a counselor at the Justice Ministry's International Department, noted that even when witnesses' testimony in court differs from their original written statement, the court (that is, the judge) can accept the original written statement given to the prosecutor. Harada goes on to state that even if a witness later refuses to testify, dies, or disappears, his statement is still acceptable to the court.

Kirk notes another aspect of the Japanese system that would appear dubious to residents of countries that stress the rights of defendants, namely, that perhaps the biggest advantage enjoyed by law enforcement authorities in Japan is that they can hold a suspect without bail for up to twenty-three days before the prosecutor decides whether or not he has enough evidence for an indictment.

George Koshi, in his excellent interpretation and description of Japanese law entitled *The Japanese Legal Advisor: Crimes and Punishments*, describes the basic steps in the investigatory process, which may include the twenty-three days of detention. This book, among other things, offers a clear guide to Japanese law for the Western lay person. At the arrest stage, a "warrant of arrest" is issued. While Koshi notes that there is a right of citizen's arrest, typically a police officer (although occasionally a public prosecutor) makes the arrest on a "warrant issued by a competent judicial authority." Fujiwara also provides a description of the arrest stage in outline form:

Arrest

(a) ordinary arrest (Art. 199)—arrest with warrant issued by a judge

1) reasonable cause enough to suspect that an offense has been committed by the suspect

2) necessity for arrest

a) danger of escape

b) danger of destruction of evidence

(b) emergency arrest (Art. 210)

1) an offense punishable by three years imprisonment or heavier punishment

2) because of great urgency, a warrant of arrest cannot be obtained beforehand

3) a warrant of arrest issued by a judge after the arrest

If a warrant of arrest is not issued, the suspect must be released immediately.

(c) flagrant arrest (Art. 212, 213)

1) flagrant offender

2) any person may arrest a flagrant offender without warrant [10]

In minor offenses punishable by a fine (cited as ¥25,000 in 1970 by Koshi) or by penal detention not exceeding thirty days, the suspect may not be arrested. However, if his name or dwelling is unknown, or if he has previously failed to appear, he may not be released. The actual warrant must include the name and address of the suspect, the nature of the alleged offense, and the facts surrounding its commission.

As is the case in the United States, when a person is arrested, he or she must immediately be informed of the reason for the arrest and the right to obtain a defense counsel of his or her own choosing. Also, the suspect is notified of the right to remain silent. As already noted, if there is not sufficient reason to detain the suspect, he or she must be released.

However, if the investigation indicates that continued detention is necessary, control over the suspect must be transferred to the public prosecutor's office within forty-eight hours of the arrest. At that point, the prosecutor's office has twenty-four hours in which to make an initial investigation and either obtain a "warrant of detention" or release the person. While Koshi notes that "In no case can a suspect be detained beyond this total period of 72 hours without a warrant of detention issued by a competent court,"[11] he points out that the court can require a further detention of ten days and that in some cases an additional ten days of detention may be granted. In a highly unusual case involving serious "crimes against the sovereignty of the nation" or "insurrection," the detention period may be extended by five days. Furthermore, several practicing lawyers have informed me that while the accused is notified of his right to counsel, access is minimal. Lawyers are given very limited time to confer with their clients during this detention period. B. J. George addressed this question at the above-mentioned Japan Society seminar on prosecutorial discretion:

> The appearance, if not the substance, of justice also might be promoted if defense counsel were permitted by law to be present during police or prosecutorial questioning upon a suspect's request.[12]

A private attorney who has acted as defense counsel in numerous cases offered this view: "In principle the law allows the accused the right to retain defense counsel, but in actual practice this may mean two or three interviews (one hour each maximum, but typically only twenty to thirty minutes each) during a ten-day period of detention. Even that limited access could be denied if it hampers the on-going investigation." Another criminal attorney, Tasuku Matsuo, indicated that his colleagues spent most of their time arguing for reduced sentences in cases rather than attempting to win acquittals (Kirk, 1981).

As Koshi observes, the issue of detention is closely connected with the question of bail:

> Request for release on bail may be made by the accused or by his attorney, wife, member of the family, or his relative, in his behalf. Where request for release on bail is made, the court is under statutory obligation to grant the bail, except (1) when the accused is charged with an offense punishable by death, imprisonment for life, or imprisonment for a minimum period of more than one year; (2) when the accused has previously been convicted of an offense punishable with a death penalty, imprisonment for life, or imprisonment for a minimum period of more than ten years; (3) when the accused has habitually committed offenses punishable with imprisonment for a maximum period of three years or more; (4) when there is reason to suspect that he may destroy evidence; (5) when there is reason to suspect that he may do harm to a person considered to be necessary for trial or to a relative of such a person; or (6) when the name or dwelling of the accused is unknown. In all other cases, the accused must be released. In certain instances, the court may grant release with or without bail on its own motion (Articles 88, 89, 91, and 95, Code of Criminal Procedure).[13]

Koshi notes that there are two problems with the application of bail. First, there is no bail bond system since there are no commercial bonding companies in Japan. Therefore, all bail must be put up in cash or "negotiable instruments" by the accused or family

Table 4

Time Required to Dispose of Cases—Japanese Public Prosecutors (1978)

	Total	Within 15 days	Within 1 month	Within 2 months	Within 3 months	Within 6 months	Within 1 year	Within 2 years	More than 2 years
Total	100 (530,617)	68.6	16.0	6.5	2.6	3.2	2.2	0.8	0.1
Cases sent from the police	100 (521,199)	69.4	16.2	6.5	2.5	3.0	1.9	0.6	0.1
Cases initiated by public prosecutors	100 (9,418)	23.9	5.0	10.5	7.8	15.2	18.2	15.2	4.3

Note 1. Traffic accident cases and traffic violations are excluded.
Note 2. Figures in the parentheses are actual numbers.
Source: Fujiwara, *op. cit.,* p. 9.

or friends. Secondly, while the bail is set by the court in an amount deemed sufficient to insure the appearance of the accused in a court hearing (taking into account the various circumstances of the case), he or she is not eligible to apply for bail until there is an indictment. Consequently, the accused cannot receive bail during the period of pre-trial detention, which can be rather lengthy as already noted.

Both Japan and America legally endorse the right to a "speedy trial." Despite these laws, the pre-trial detention for America's accused is so notoriously long that it needs no elaboration here. In Japan, a speedy trial is achieved in the great majority of cases, as evidenced by the fact that eighty to ninety percent of criminal cases are disposed of within six months (Tsuchiya, 1980).

Fujiwara provides a more detailed look at the time frame involved in the disposition of cases processed by Japanese public prosecutors (Table 4).

The cases handled by the public prosecutor are subject to the following exceptions:

> 1. In juvenile cases the family court has the authority to decide whether or not to prosecute.
> 2. Minor traffic violations are exempted. These cases are handled by police under what is referred to as the *hansoku-kin* system.
> 3. Trivial cases designated by the public prosecutor. In 1978, 19.1 percent of all Penal Code cases or 72,749 cases were so defined. Examples include an instance in which the value of stolen goods was less than 5000 yen ($25), or the theft of a bicycle which was worth 5000 yen or less.[14]

Another method used by public prosecutors is referred to as "summary procedure." Minor charges are disposed of with modest fines (less than ¥200,000, or about $1,000) and without public hearings. Also, when a "summary procedure" is instituted, the defendant does not have to appear in court. The "summary procedure" is usually employed in cases where there is no dispute regarding the facts. A very large majority (99.3 percent) of "violation of the road law" cases are disposed of in this manner. The prosecutor

Table 5
Disposition of Cases by Public Prosecutors (1978)

		Total	Penal Code offenses	Violation of the Road Traffic Law	Other special law offenses
	Cases referred to the public prosecutor from the police officer	3,294,245	841,926	2,308,157	144,162
Disposition by the public prosecutor	Total	4,553,075	1,107,455	3,230,523	215,097
	Prosecution	(88.6%)	(64.4%)	(97.1%)	(74.5%)
	sub-total	2,572,221	427,390	2,040,445	104,386
	formal trial	146,112 (5.7%)	97,917 (22.9%)	14,732 (0.7%)	33,463 (32.1%)
	summary procedure	2,426,109 (94.3%)	329,473 (77.1%)	2,025,713 (99.3%)	70,923 (67.9%)
	Non-Prosecution sub-total	(11.4%) 332,157	(35.6%) 235,995	(2.9%) 60,481	(25.5%) 35,681
	suspension of prosecution	265,312 (9.1%)	183,074 (27.6%)	52,825 (2.5%)	29,413 (21.0%)
	others	66,826	52,921	7,656	6,249
	Referral to Family Court	455,905	186,315	263,415	6,175
	Stay of disposition	1,192,792	257,755	866,182	68,855

Source: Fujiwara, *op. cit.*, p. 10.

recommends to the court that a certain case be disposed of by means of "summary procedure," but the judge need not agree and can refer the case for public trial. An overall look at the disposition of cases by public prosecutors during 1978 is offered by Fujiwara and is reproduced here (Table 5).

While "double jeopardy" is prohibited by law at the trial level in Japan, the prosecutor may appeal factual or legal issues as well as the sentence itself, and in instances where the sentence differs markedly from the one recommended by the prosecutor, appeals are common. In 1978, the prosecution was successful in 75.6 percent of all its appeals.

As a balance of the above view on the role of the prosecution in the Japanese system of justice, it should be noted that remedies are available for prosecutorial abuse. Yoshio Suzuki addressed this issue in the above-mentioned 1980 Japan Society seminar by discussing two other features of the Japanese system, the "Inquest of Prosecution" and the "Analogical Institution of Prosecution." Briefly, the former involves a commission composed of eleven local voters chosen at random for six-month terms which is attached to each district court. A victim or complainant may raise the issue that "prosecution was improperly declined," and then the commission will conduct its own investigation based on case records and the examination of witnesses. If the commission decides that the criminal should have been prosecuted, the chief public prosecutor must reconsider the case, but he still retains the right to prosecute or not. The "Analogical Institution of Prosecution" is an approach that is designed to counter any prejudice or bias of prosecutors. It attempts to prevent any appearance of impropriety where public officials are accused of abusing their power. It also has jurisdiction over charges of police brutality and abuses by other justice personnel. The approach is similar to that of the appointment of a special prosecutor in the United States. Action is initiated by a victim or complainant as in the case of the "Inquest of Prosecution," and the court conducts an independent inquiry. If the court decides prosecution should be undertaken, then a private attorney is appointed in place of the prosecutor.

Use of Informants by the Police
One more feature of criminal investigation by the police themselves is worthy of note. According to Ames (1981), investigations conducted by police detectives use informants, or *kyōryokusha*. Initial routine investigations are handled by *kōban* police, but more serious problems are dealt with by specialists. In the case of criminal investigations, detectives assigned to the nearest station become involved. Like investigators in most countries, their ability to "cultivate the field," or develop working relationships with local

individuals, including ex-offenders, is closely related to their success. The people who act as informants and tipsters include bar hostesses, bar operators, managers of rooming houses, *pachinko* hall operators, and pawnshop proprietors. Ames's description of the task of the detective (*keiji*) is informative:

> Young *keiji* are exhorted to enlarge their "field" because "if the field is large, then the harvest is large" (Criminal Investigator, Kurashiki Police Station, 1974). Detectives spend a large part of their time visiting with their tipsters (called *kyōryokusha*, "co-operators") to deepen their personal bonds of friendship and obligation (*giri*). Whenever there is a death in the family of a tipster, a marriage, or any other event the *keiji* always comes with an appropriate gift to symbolize the relationship. Cultivating the field involves spending a large amount of off-duty time with many *kyōryokusha*, usually at night, drinking, playing Mah-Jongg, and the like. The *keiji* work hard to build relationships of mutual confidence so that the tipster will provide information should he or she become aware of a crime.[15]

With this groundwork laid by the *keiji* and the broad powers of the prosecutor, the Western observer begins to understand the reasons for the effectiveness of the Japanese justice system. Another factor is the dedication of police officers at all levels, and I will examine this and other attitudes of the police in the next chapter.

NOTES
1. U.S. Department of Justice, *F.B.I. Uniform Crime Reports—Crime in the United States, 1979* (Washington, D.C.: U.S. Government Printing Office, 1980), p. 177.
2. B. Basler, "McGuire Appraises Police and Outlines Some Goals," *The New York Times*, June 9, 1981, p. B8.
3. *Ibid.*
4. The Japan Society, " The Role of Public Prosecutors in Criminal Justice: Prosecutorial Discretion in Japan and the United States." A Seminar Report, *Public Affairs Series* 14, New York, September 15, 1980, p. 5.
5. William Clifford, *Crime Control in Japan* (Lexington, Massachusetts: Lexington Books, 1976), p. 67.
6. H. Tanaka, *The Japanese Legal System: Introductory Cases and Materials* (Tokyo: University of Tokyo Press, 1976), pp. 261–62.

7. A. Nagashima, "The Accused and Society: The Administration of Criminal Justice in Japan." In A. Von Mehren, ed., *Law in Japan: The Legal Order in a Changing Society* (Cambridge, Massachusetts: Harvard University Press, 1963), p. 299.

8. Japan Society, *op. cit.*, p. 8.

9. T. Fujiwara, presentation entitled "Criminal Justice System in Japan (III): Criminal Investigation." Unpublished, mimeographed paper, the United Nations Asia and Far East Institute for the Prevention of Crime and Treatment of Offenders, Tokyo, fall, 1980, p. 8. (Mr. Fujiwara is a public prosecutor currently on the staff of the above-mentioned institute.)

10. *Ibid.*, p. 5.

11. George M. Koshi, *The Japanese Legal Advisor: Crimes and Punishments* (Tokyo and Rutland, Vermont: Charles E. Tuttle, 1970), p. 76.

12. Japan Society, *op. cit.*, p. 20.

13. Koshi, *op. cit.*, p. 77.

14. Fujiwara, *op. cit.*, p. 2.

15. Walter L. Ames, *Police and Community in Japan* (Berkeley, California: University of California Press, 1981), p. 131.

Chapter 6

ATTITUDES OF THE POLICE TOWARD THEIR WORK

During visits to *kōban* and *chūzaisho*, there was ample time to talk with police officers about their attitudes toward their work, including how they became interested in their occupation, and their perceptions of the future of police–community relations. Occasionally I made inquiries about discipline problems, weaknesses within the organization, and how family members felt about their employment as police officers. For instance, the changing shift pattern of American police officers has been such an irritant for spouses that it is often attributed to be one of the causes of divorce. I was interested to know whether the Japanese police experience similar difficulties.

These conversations at police boxes were with "street-level" officers, usually those holding the rank of policeman, senior policeman, sergeant, or assistant inspector. However, I also discussed these topics with higher-ranking personnel, including members of the elite police—those who had entered as assistant inspectors. Usually they were administrators working out of the headquarters of the National Police Agency, the Tokyo Metropolitan Police Department, the Hokkaido Prefectural Police Office, and so on. Some were superintendents, others senior superintendents and occasionally even higher-ranking personnel at the apex of the administrative hierarchy. Meetings with these top-level officials were somewhat different in tone and often proved to be events in their own right. I particularly remember a luncheon with a chief police superintendent who was second-in-command at a prefectural police agency. I was given the red carpet treatment, complete with a chauffeur-driven trip to an expensive restaurant nearby. Information gathered from high-ranking as well as low-ranking personnel was supplemented by contacts with other justice personnel and private citizens who helped to deepen my understanding of the attitudes of the police toward their work.

Street Police

As mentioned earlier, I attempted to create an informal atmosphere in my conversations at police boxes, and the flow of conversation was far more important to me than adhering rigidly to a prearranged set of questions. Responses, of course, varied tremendously, and occasionally avenues of discussion opened up that were totally unanticipated. Frequently I had the luxury of time on my side—I usually spent a full day at a police box. Unless the police were unusually busy, there was ample time for conversation. This portion of my research was decidedly dependent on the candidness of the officers interviewed and on my ability to establish a rapport.

Given this background, I have selected the following excerpts from interviews, which I believe help to capture the flavor of the encounters and the attitudes of these men toward their work. The information seems to lend itself to this narrative style as opposed to a survey approach in which data are categorized and presented in tabular form. While the latter approach has the advantage of presenting a large amount of material in a concise manner, it fails to convey the subtleties and nuances of individual answers to specific questions. For those interested in the more quantitative approach I recommend the data gathered by the Okayama Prefectural Police and reported by Ames in *Police and Community in Japan.*

How They Became Interested

As is the case in the United States, it appears that aspiring young officers in Japan begin with notions of becoming detectives and investigating crime. Television programs and films, imported and domestic, glamorize the role of the detective. An officer who was approaching retirement and who worked out of the Tsukiji *kō-*

ban in Tokyo mentioned this as the reason for his original interest in joining. He noted that while he felt disappointment over never having become a detective, he nevertheless enjoyed the contacts with citizens in his day-to-day work at the *kōban*.

A sergeant at a *kōban* in the Akabane area of Tokyo had been a police officer for thirty years. He noted that he became interested in police work at the close of the Second World War, when "life was a mess" and few jobs were available. He said that, "Despite the hierarchical paramilitary structure of the police force and the strict discipline, younger people who enter now speak more frankly and occasionally with humor to their superiors." I countered with, "Don't you lose discipline in a more relaxed system?" To which he responded, "Yes, but working in a police box is more like working in a family setting. It's not that I command them." When I asked if he could generalize about these attitudes, he remarked, "Well, of course it is difficult, but practically speaking (and perhaps inevitably) living overnight here at the *kōban* creates an environment that encourages close working relationships." At another point, he was nostalgic for an earlier period: "Obedience still characterizes the attitudes of older citizens toward police, even if they tasted the fear of the earlier prewar period, while young people are not particularly obedient. Routine visits used to be done, and the families known thoroughly. We used to have much more knowledge—very complete—but now there is just a brief visit. For example, if a woman lost her husband during the war, she would talk to police about it and feel gratitude for the assistance she received. Also, during that period they had a relationship more like that of friends and today that has been lessened, but there is still a carry-over."

A problem concerning the future of policing that was raised on a number of occasions by different officers was also voiced. "There are a group of us [in the Tokyo M.P.D.], around six thousand in number, who have worked for around thirty years and who are rapidly approaching retirement. There is concern about the void in police skills that will exist when we leave."

Finally, concerning the demands of the job, he said that it is both physically and psychologically less taxing than it used to be.

Table 6

Reasons Given for Joining the Police in Okayama Prefecture

	College graduates (Total: 140)	High school graduates (Total: 102)	Total (242)
To serve society	20.0	15.7	18.2
Because it is a stable life	14.3	23.5	18.2
Because of an advancement examination system based on ability	25.7	8.8	18.6
Because it is a good job for a man	28.6	38.3	32.6
Was attracted by the uniform	0.7	0.0	0.4
No other suitable job available	2.1	4.9	3.3
Wanted to ride a patrol car or motorcycle	0.0	2.9	1.2
Other	8.6	5.9	7.4

Source: Walter L. Ames, *Police and Community in Japan* (Berkeley, California: University of California Press, 1981), p. 166.

The shift patterns that were adopted after the Second World War, which imitated the American system, were quickly abandoned in favor of the present four-day pattern described earlier. Furthermore, in recent years there has been less emotional tension compared to the previous decade, when political dissidents were active.

It was not uncommon to hear officers talk about the "stability" of police work as a factor in their choice of an occupation. One thirty-year senior policeman mentioned this as his main reason for joining. In addition to being attracted by stability, he had been encouraged to join by his *sensei* (teacher or mentor), and he had ruled out a desk job.

While the economic conditions of different periods of Japanese history have affected the recruitment process, stability was still an important factor for younger officers even in the prosperous seventies, as Ames's data shows. In 1974, 18.2 percent of recruits offered this as a reason for joining. The responses offered by recruits from Ames's research in Okayama are shown in Table 6.

Unlike Tokyo, where a large majority of police are recruited from outside the prefecture, 98 percent of Okayama's officers had lived in the prefecture. Despite this difference in recruitment, however, it is probable that the responses of the Okayama police can be considered representative of the force as a whole. Of 312 applicants who took the police entrance examination in Okayama in 1974, the following answers were given to the question of who had urged them to join the police: family, 24 percent; relative or friend, 8.7 percent; teacher, 3.8 percent; and police officer, 48.1 percent.[1]

Data gathered by police on Japan's northernmost island of Hokkaido concerning the reasons for joining the police agency resemble that recorded by Okayama authorities. The vice chief of the Patrol Division of the Hokkaido Prefectural Police mentioned the following reasons (according to frequency): 1. Being a policeman is a manly job; 2. Police stand on the side of justice and punish criminals; 3. The income is steady.

Another sergeant, fifty-seven years old, who was working out of a *kōban* in the Seijō station area of Tokyo, also entered police work immediately after the Second World War. He made similar comments on the disorder that existed in Japan at that time, limiting his choice of occupation. Raised in Fukushima Prefecture, he attended school in Tokyo. For him, retirement was just six months away, and although his retirement plans were vague, he wanted to do something active to keep him healthy. The job was physically demanding, and kendo had helped him maintain his physical condition.

A younger officer, aged thirty-four, shared the assignment at the same police box in this outlying area of Tokyo. Raised in Hokkaido, he was attracted to police work because he liked judo. Proud of his physical prowess, he said, "I never lost a fight when I was growing up." He worked on his parents' dairy farm until he reached the age of eighteen. His wife, like those of most officers, accepts her husband's choice of occupation, but it is unclear to what extent this represents mere acquiescence or more positive acceptance. A Japanese wife would be expected to support her husband's choice of occupation to a greater extent than her more outspoken counterpart in the United States. Notwithstanding his self-confessed combativeness at an earlier age, he said he had never drawn his firearm. He recounted one incident, eight years earlier, when he was called to a family quarrel where the father was drunk and wildly swinging a sword, frightening family members. He had been required to disarm the man, but even on that occasion he had done this without resorting to the use of his gun. His greatest job satisfaction, he indicated, was "being of assistance to others," while having to "sit around" was clearly the most boring feature of his work. Like many officers, he took pride in his work and observed that police work tended to remain free of corruption generally because officers were "obedient and faithful" to their job. This last comment reflects the *esprit de corps* and the high performance standards of Japanese police.

One rugged, thirty-seven-year-old sergeant, assigned to a *kōban* just three years previously, had spent six years with the riot police, or *kidōtai*. Earlier, he had been assigned to the Traffic Information Center at the headquarters of the Tokyo Metropolitan Police Department. His responses to my questions were short and clipped, as if he were determined to meet only the minimal professional requirements of the situation. Nonetheless some information emerged. "Police work is clean work; it's good for a man. It's also a special type of service work that, unlike other public service jobs, demands more activity—it's not desk work." ("It's good for a man" reflects the popular image of what police work is like, and this was by far the most frequently given reason for wanting to join the police force in Okayama Prefecture—32.6 percent of applicants mentioned it.)

Work with the *kidōtai* was difficult during the sixties when students were on the rampage, and he admitted having been frightened on one occasion when the windshield of his car was smashed. Like most riot police, he was unmarried at the time, but out-of-town assignments and the constant readiness had still been a chore. The high level of physical training was one of the more enjoyable features. Most *kidōtai* officers are rotated out of that duty every three years, but he had spent six years in the assignment as a mechanic working on the various types of vehicles required by this paramilitary unit. As one learns about and observes units of the *kidōtai* during street demonstrations, a comparison with U.S. Army National Guard becomes inevitable. The National Guard unit also operates independently, and its methods, including training, are militaristic, but the comparison only goes so far; Army National Guard units are not nearly as well-trained or disciplined as the *kidōtai*. Ames spent time with one of the *kidōtai* units in Tokyo and his comments are illuminating. He goes so far as to say that the organization is "modeled directly after the abolished Imperial Japanese Army" and that the "Way of the Warrior" (the samurai ethic) is exemplified in the riot police.

Another sergeant I interviewed had been a member of the Japanese Self-Defense Force before joining the police. The term "Self-Defense Force" is a euphemism for the armed forces as Japan's post–Second World War constitution does not permit the development of an offensive military machine. He decided to join the police force because prior military service allowed him to start with a high salary. He confessed that prior to joining he had worked as a "public officer"—a person who investigates communists.

An older veteran of the Tokyo M.P.D. revealed an incident that had drawn him to policing as an occupation. As a youngster, he had been raised on a farm in Okayama Prefecture before joining the army during the Second World War. After a bombing raid near Osaka, he and an uncle were assisting two children who were in "bad shape." Apparently disoriented, the children were crying and hungry. They met a police officer, who arranged shelter for the children and gave them food. This act of kindness, which was in sharp contrast to his image of police as authoritarian, was primarily responsible for his decision to become a police officer.

Family ties to police work were not infrequently mentioned as being responsible for interest in the occupation. This reason was cited by two officers, one young and one middle aged, assigned to a *kōban* in Sapporo. In one case, a grandfather had been in police work, while in the other a friend's father who was a police officer had encouraged him to take the examination. Another Hokkaido officer, from the Asahikawa area, had become interested in police work because his father worked for the Hokkaido Prefectural Police. One sergeant in Tokyo said, "When I was small, my grandfather and uncle were policemen, mainly that was it."

One young officer at a *chuzaisho* on the outskirts of Tokyo noted that "a sense of justice" had contributed to his choice of police work. This thirty-one-year-old senior policeman had witnessed the student uprisings of the sixties in which barricades had been erected on his college campus. Unlike some of his friends who sympathized with the demonstrators, he felt angry when many classes were canceled:"It didn't seem fair." This contributed to his desire to become a policeman.

One young, recently promoted sergeant in his thirties whom I met at a police box in Tokyo became a good friend. He was the first officer I spoke with after my arrival in Japan, before I had officially commenced my research. It was a chance meeting: I had asked for directions at a police box where the officer could not speak English, and this man, stationed at a neighboring police box a mile or two away, was phoned. This downtown area of Tokyo is frequented by foreigners, and most inquiries from English-speaking visitors are referred to this man when he is on duty.

After a few minutes of conversation, I was amazed to discover that he had read Bayley's book, *Forces of Order: Police Behavior in Japan and the United States*, and so I eagerly sought his impressions. The book was accurate in his opinion; he indicated that many Tokyo police had read the Japanese translation. Not only had he read Bayley, but he was eager to learn of other American criminological works. On a piece of paper he had scrawled the title of a sociological text by Walter Reckless, a well-known American scholar. His lively intellect and interest in American police practices contributed to a friendship that was to evolve over the ensuing months.

His English is excellent, which is rare among Japanese street police. Some members of the higher-ranking police of both the National Police Agency and the Tokyo Metropolitan Police Department speak English fairly well, but it is unusual to find such a fluent street-level officer. He graduated from college with a degree in engineering and then worked in the sales department of a Japanese firm that specializes in international business. This permitted him to travel to other Asian countries. Several years later, he left and joined the M.P.D. Like other Japanese, he had received some exposure to English during junior high school, but this did not explain his fluency. He credited this ability to having listened to the U.S. Armed Forces radio station, which broadcasts programs in Tokyo.

While he thoroughly enjoyed his work, his wife found it a bit taxing to adjust to his hours. His police box, like many others, was pleasantly decorated with flowers. Like most police, he took a gentle, low-keyed approach with drunks—there were many wandering the streets in his section of Tokyo after 11 P.M.

He confirmed Bayley's view that womanizing and drinking and driving occasionally present a discipline problem among police, but he added that if an officer loses his police identification card, disciplinary action can follow. Serious disciplinary problems, however, are rare. In one instance he knew of, an officer had an affair with a married woman in the neighborhood of his *kōban*. The ensuing gossip and complaints registered with his superiors resulted in his transfer to a different *kōban* and a reprimand. Noting that while businessmen engage in a fair amount of extramarital activity, he hazarded a guess that few policemen do. Officers are frequently reminded about their conduct by superiors. One weekend when he was among a group of thirty police headed out of town for a vacation trip, they were, he said, "preached at not to get into trouble." Some of the group complained, "They treat us like children."

More serious acts by police, including criminal offenses, while less frequent in Japan than in the United States, are occasionally reported in the press. Four examples follow.

Arrested for stealing goods from a supermarket, a forty-two-year-old police inspector, who was chief of the crime prevention section of a police station in Chiba, was "discharged in disgrace." He had attempted to blame the shoplifting on his eleven-year-old daughter until eyewitnesses forced him to admit to the crime. He had picked up three cassette music tapes worth ¥12,000 ($50).

A former police inspector was arrested for robbing a credit union of ¥500,000 ($2,200) in Yokohama. Police reported that a masked man, "brandishing a kitchen knife," broke into a branch of the Yokohama Dai-Ichi Credit Union and threatened a teller with a knife. The credit union immediately telephoned the police, while three employees armed with wooden swords chased after the thief.

In 1982, there was a rare case of alleged corruption at higher levels of the police force. The man who had been the head of the Osaka Prefectural Police at the time of the incident killed himself, a typically Japanese suicide in which he assumed responsibility for the wrongdoing. While he had been reassigned as the director of the Police Academy before the corruption case unfolded and while there was no indication that he was directly involved, he nonetheless took responsibility for not having prevented it.

In a different vein, a thirty-three-year-old detective of the Fukuoka Prefectural Police was accused of having "intimate relations" with the wife of a local gang leader and receiving ¥4 million ($18,000) from her. He had become acquainted with her at a snack bar and borrowed money from her to repay the loan he had obtained to buy a ¥12 million ($50,000) condominium. The officer was suspended pending further investigation. Fukuoka Prefecture has been one of the most active areas for gangsters, and police claim that 3,200 gangsters are associated with 144 underground organizations in the prefecture. The officer involved had investigated 600 gangsters in 40 gangs. Ames (1981) provides a closer look at the relationships between police and gangsters.

Returning to the sketches of street police, in one police box I interviewed three officers together, and asked them how they had become interested in the police. One was from Kyushu, in the south of Japan. His family was poor and he came to Tokyo for a college education. He dropped out, and police work became one of the few available jobs he could find in a tight job market. The second officer grew up on a farm as the oldest son but found farming dull. Police work seemed exciting, so he left the farm. The third officer said he had consulted a Buddhist priest. He had a vague notion that policemen were relied upon by people. The priest supported his interest in this aspect of police work and he subsequently joined. When asked what jobs they would seek now if required to choose alternative careers, they mentioned Buddhist priest, teacher, and farmer, respectively.

Officers are not immune to verbal abuse although they generally receive much less than their American counterparts. One policeman, who seemed a bit unhappy with his choice of career, said, "There is a kind of obligation around your neck. When local teenagers hurl bad names or insults, you can't talk back." He said, "I've been called '*bakayarō*' [you dumb jerk] and '*wakazō*' [the equivalent of 'punk' or 'kid,' implying a lack of maturity]. Often when people are drunk, they say, 'Why do I have to get bossed around by a punk kid?' "

The fact that "service to the public" links occupational interests as diverse as law enforcement and teaching is revealed in one officer's comments. "I got interested in police work because 'service' runs in the family. My parents were teachers and other relatives worked for various governmental agencies, and therefore it seemed natural to go into police work."

Problems and Future Prospects

I sometimes asked lower-ranking police about problem areas within police work, including organizational weaknesses. Naturally, they were not always eager to specify things they were dissatisfied with or identify problems within the police agency. Occasionally, I managed to "tease out" criticisms. Sometimes I linked this discussion with inquiries concerning future problems and prospects facing the police. A number of officers provided perceptive and thoughtful answers.

One *chūzai-san* from Hokkaido linked the frequently mentioned issue of citizens citing their "rights" with a growing sense of individuality and social distance among the people in his village.

> People feel freer to argue with police. But in town associations, too, there is an increasing reluctance to serve others. Compared to ten years ago, people seem to lack a spirit of cooperation, not only toward the police but among themselves. This tendency will increase in the years ahead,

which will make it difficult for police to do their work. In order to inspire cooperation, we will have to make a greater effort. For example, we were trying to catch a man who was making explosives in his apartment, but his next-door neighbors "didn't know about it." We had been working with the local TV station on it, yet the growing distance among Japanese prevented us from getting help from this criminal's neighbors.

One assistant inspector in his early forties who had worked undercover was concerned about the problem of ferreting out radical students. The dissidents are fewer in number these days, and the main difficulty comes from violent infighting between extremist groups such as the *Chūkakuha* and *Kakumaruha*. The police have been unable to penetrate their ranks and break them up. Another officer also addressed the problem of radical students, observing, "There is a cyclical aspect to student riots. When the Japanese Security Treaty with America comes up for renewal, there's a potential for new riots."

An officer at a Motofuji area police box in Tokyo mentioned two problem areas for police. The first, traffic enforcement, is of concern to administrators as well. Officers on traffic detail are sometimes accused by *kōban* police of over-zealous enforcement of the law. He acknowledged that a balance is required and commented:

As you know, it is important to maintain good communications between officers and the surrounding community. Traffic is regulated by the traffic section, and sometimes by the patrol department. The possibility of hostile reactions by the public mostly arises because the traffic section too strictly enforces the code. One example is illegal parking. But in most cases when citizens are warned, they go home with the realization that they have done something wrong. Therefore, it isn't just a matter of resentment directed toward the police.

A future concern for police, he believed, was the rise in juvenile delinquency. "The fact is that the age is dropping—it used to be high school students, but now it's junior high school students. Some are very dangerous prospective criminals."

Some responses to questions about future prospects and improvements needed in police work yielded statements reminiscent of American police. A detective in the Shitaya station area responded, "We need to expand the size of the police force to deal with growing criminality." While police in the United States might agree, scholars and students of policing have become increasingly skeptical of this stock response, and with good reason. A study conducted by the Police Foundation found that saturating an area in Kansas City with police patrols was not effective in reducing crime, and that a comparable region of the city with a minimal police presence had similar crime rates.

This M.P.D. detective went on to note that officers like himself are sometimes unhappy with the limitations imposed upon them when they interrogate suspects. He added another complaint: "Some officers with ability feel too much emphasis is placed on the paper exam, which restricts their opportunities for promotion."

Occasionally officers expressed concern about the planning for and the management of earthquake-related problems. One superintendent stated that this issue was currently being studied by high-ranking officials. The citizens of Tokyo, at least, are understandably concerned about a possible repeat of the 1923 quake that devastated the city. A major quake has been forecast for this region of Japan, and the number of minor earthquakes are an ever-present reminder of potential devastation.

Police Administrators

Not surprisingly, a different pattern of vocational and professional interests characterizes many of the higher-ranking officers. There are two groups: those who have risen through the ranks to inspector, superintendent, or higher, and those who are identified from the outset as elite, having entered as assistant inspectors. The latter, as previously mentioned, are frequently graduates of Tokyo University's law department. Many of the superintendents and inspector-level middle managers I met were part of the elite group of those who had passed the National Public Service Examination. Some of this elite had considered other public service careers (the ministries compete for the most able graduates from the most prestigious universities) before joining the National Police Agency. Unlike the street-level police, few had family members in police work.

All who do manage to enter as assistant inspectors are marked for top careers with the National Police Agency. Many will rise to become chiefs of the forty-seven prefectural police agencies. Some will graduate into high-level positions within the headquarters of the National Police Agency in Tokyo, while others will be posted to Japanese embassies overseas. It is very difficult to enter, but once one has done so one can feel secure. It is rare for a person to be fired, mediocre job performance notwithstanding. If a person is not performing well, he will be shifted to a different position.

Promotions in the police, except at the top levels, are on a very regular basis, and an officer keeps pace for the most part with his "classmates." Entering bureaucrats are very conscious of colleagues who enter at the same time, and a sense of camaraderie often develops among them. Salary increases and regular bonuses that are given out twice annually, as in industry, are generally similar, and neither salary increases nor bonuses are linked to meritorious performance, contrary to the practice in the United States.

Officers I became acquainted with were talented and versatile. I was impressed by their strong educational backgrounds, broad-mindedness, and general intelligence. While several admitted that they would like to have had careers in law, they had been unable to pass the entrance examination for the Judicial and Legal Training Institute. As mentioned earlier, thirty thousand applicants annually seek admission to this training institute, which accepts just five hundred. Moreover, just ten to twenty individuals are selected annually to become assistant inspectors in the National Police Agency's program to train and develop top managers. As in industry, the large majority of entering recruits will continue with the police agency throughout their careers. In Japan, management-level positions in the national ministries and agencies carry more prestige than do similar positions in private industry, the converse of the situation in the United States.

One inspector impressed me especially. His intellectual approach and willingness to confront problem areas with a visiting researcher struck me the first day we met. He discussed police work candidly and commented on Bayley's book, which was at the time the only Western publication on Japanese policing. With a good command of English, he had a knack for effectively conveying his analysis of an issue. Still in his twenties, he had been a police officer for approximately two years. Asked about career goals, he indicated that he hoped to become the "First Officer" at some embassy abroad.

At the outset of his career, after completing the mandatory three months of training at the National Police Academy, he was given an additional six-month field training assignment. Typical of other elite officers, he was given supervisory responsibility over a group of street police at a station in Aichi Prefecture, an opportunity for newcomers to get a feeling for grass roots policing.

He noted that attitudes of young patrol police have changed, as evidenced by the fact that today officers desiring promotion spend time studying materials published monthly by the National Police Agency. During an earlier era, one avenue for promotion consisted of impressing one's superior through effective off-duty work. This took the form of intelligence gathering—for example, trying to get in with the head of a neighborhood group (chōnaikai). Older officers sometimes viewed with disdain younger officers who failed to devote off-duty hours to police work.

National Police Agency administrators were divided, he noted, over the merits of changing the retirement age from fifty-five to sixty. While he recognized the arduousness of police work, particularly for patrol personnel, he felt a sixty-year-old retirement age would offer an extended period of good income. Presently, officers receive relatively low retirement pay.

From his perspective in the Safety Bureau of the National Police Agency, gangsters present the most serious problem facing police in the immediate future. The Safety Bureau is charged with drug enforcement and the investigation of white-collar crime, and it coordinates policy in these fields for the entire country. At the time we were discussing these issues, he had been asked to generate a plan for a public media campaign to deal with increased stimulant use among young people. I asked if he could rely on other National Police Agency officials for assistance, which led to a discussion of factionalism and its impact on decision making. Workers are prohibited from seeking assistance from offices outside their bureaus.

A police superintendent working at the National Police Academy told me he was also a Tokyo University graduate, but, unable to gain admission to the Judicial and Legal Training Institute to become a lawyer, he had chosen police work because of its uniformed status. Noting that if he had chosen to enter the Self-Defense Force, it would have been among the non-uniformed ranks, he confessed to finding the uniform attractive. After completing the Training Academy program, he was assigned to supervise ten experienced men in the field, a difficult task for an inexperienced assistant inspector. Later, he worked in the Traffic Division for several years and then in "public security" (a euphemism for intelligence work), which involved gathering information on student radicals. Like his middle-management colleagues, he seemed intelligent and highly professional.

Discussing disciplinary problems, he mentioned that sometimes officers are required to appear before a committee of supervisory personnel. In the case of drinking or "women" problems, an officer's supervisor might suggest that he resign. If the person balked at this, he could be assigned to trifling jobs with no opportunity for promotion—in effect, disgraced. More serious cases, such as shooting a suspect, might involve review by a public prosecutor.

Discussing the future, he repeated the observation that many older officers were due to retire at the same time, leaving a vacuum. Adding to the problem was the difference in attitude between older and younger police. Older police perceive "work as life itself." Younger officers take a "salaried man" point of view, that police work is a nine-to-five type of job and only the required hours are logged. He also emphasized that officers don't work during their off-duty hours "cultivating the field," as they did in earlier times.

A day spent with a chief superintendent, the second-in-command at a prefectural police agency north of Tokyo, was particularly gratifying because of the candid give-and-take conversation. Fluent in English, this maverick had studied political science at Johns Hopkins University on a Fulbright in the 1960s. I was startled to hear him challenge the efficiency of the *kōban* and *chūzaisho* system. This was practically heresy! It is not working in its present form, he claimed, because rapid urbanization creates different kinds of demands on the system. Traffic control, criminal investigation, and delinquency in schools require manpower allocation based on a centralized administration. "Currently, teams of officers go out to handle investigations and delinquency problems in schools. A single officer out of a police box cannot handle these tasks." Efficiency was a key word for him, but he acknowledged that change was difficult because local neighborhood residents are wedded to the *kōban* system. "Changing the *kōban* system quickly would bring an outcry from the public and politicians."

In a major city in his prefecture there was one policeman for every 1,900 residents. "How is it possible," he asked rhetorically, "for the officer to know everyone?" Though he was not completely without sympathizers, few other top administrators agreed with his philosophy. This prefecture, slightly to the north of Tokyo, was undergoing more rapid industrial and population growth than most, and this might have influenced his somewhat idiosyncratic attitudes toward the system. He favored phasing out at least some police boxes so that the limited manpower could be reallocated to deal with the previously mentioned problems. Needless to say, although his opinion apparently represented a minority view, that in itself did not invalidate it. Indeed, conventional thinking in any field follows those creative enough to work at the cutting edge of social change.

The working hours for these higher-ranking officers were not a standard nine-to-five routine but rather frequently included evening work and a half-day on Saturday. Some private industries have cut out Saturday work, and Japan watchers are interested to see if this will spill over into the public sector.

A superintendent in the Crime Prevention Division of the National Police Agency was particularly helpful to me. Flexible and possessing a good sense of humor, he applied himself conscientiously to his work at the agency. We had many conversations and contacts as he coordinated some of my research activities. Family background was a factor in his selection of police work; his father had worked in crime prevention at the prefectural police agency in Osaka. A graduate of Tokyo University's law department, he was a strong supporter of the *kōban* system, remarking that, "It is the only thing that makes Japanese police unique." Juvenile delinquency was the major problem facing police in the years ahead, he thought, and he cited the recent upsurge in juvenile crime to support this contention.

He and his fellow elite officers are transferred on average every one to three years and occasionally more frequently. There is a serious question as to whether these officers can attain a high level of productivity in their positions, given their short-term assignments. Comments from several lower-ranking police officers and legal scholars support such skepticism. On the other hand, one could hardly quarrel with the breadth of their training for eventual top prefectural police assignments. Furthermore, the officers themselves told me that they felt they could master a new assignment in three or four months, and that two years in one post was just about the right amount of time.

Again, Ouchi's analysis in *Theory Z* of Japanese and American business practices helps make the case for "non-specialized career paths." A number of examples are cited, but one of the advantages of this approach is offered in this description:

> In the Japanese case virtually every department will have in it someone who knows the people, the problems, and the procedure of any other area within the organization. When coordination is necessary, both sides will be able to understand and cooperate with the other. Perhaps more important is the fact that every employee knows that he will continue through his career to move between functions, offices, and geographical locations. The person from another department who

is asking for assistance today may be the person who will be his co-worker or even superior tomorrow. Thus there is not only the ability but also the incentive for taking a broad, organization-wide point of view and for cooperating with everyone.[2]

Examples of the breadth of training of upper-echelon personnel are offered in the following chronology of assignments of two elite superintendents, both in their early thirties. After graduating from the three months of training at the Police Academy, one officer was assigned to supervise *kōban* officers in a prefectural police agency to the south of Tokyo for six months. His second assignment was to a police agency in the western part of Japan for approximately eighteen months, and that was followed by a three-year commitment to the Self-Defense Force. (It is not uncommon for officers to be assigned temporarily to the military agency or even to the Japanese National Railways.) This assignment was followed by an appointment to the Crime Prevention Division with the headquarters of the National Police Agency in Tokyo for several years. Most recently, he was shifted to the Juvenile Delinquency Section of the Hokkaido Prefectural Police in Sapporo.

Another career pattern, in brief outline form, was:

—National Police Agency (Pre-service Executive Training Course for successful applicants from the National Public Service Examination) as assistant inspector: three months.

—Kyoto Prefectural Police, supervising patrol police: eight months.

—National Police Agency in Tokyo; Security Division. Assignment included investigating problems associated with left-wing infiltration of labor unions, strike activities, and the Japan Teachers Union: one year.

—National Police Agency in Tokyo; transferred to International Criminal Affairs Division (Criminal Investigation) (required two months of training in Criminal Procedural Law, National Police Academy): one and a half years.

—Kagoshima Prefectural Police; chief of criminal investigation with focus on fraud, embezzlement, and organized crime cases: one year.

—Prime Minister's Office (technically on loan); counselor, coordinating functions with other ministries and agencies: two years.

—National Police Agency in Tokyo; assistant director, Juvenile Delinquency Section, in charge of "guidance" (relationship of adults, including gangsters, to youth): three years.

One final problem should be noted. It is not easy on the personal lives of police managers to have to move every two to three years, and it can be a wretched and painful experience for wives and children. As children become older their schooling becomes extremely important, and sometimes families will decide that it is best for them to stay in a particular location while the father moves on to his new assignment. He will then return home on weekends or, if he is in a distant prefecture, he may even be forced to fly home once a month.

A personable superintendent in Kobe, assigned to the Foreign Affairs Section of the Hyōgo Prefectural Police, was very conscious of social changes taking place within Japan and pointed to the changing structure of families as contributing to weaker social controls. "We used to think of the family as grandparents as well as mother, father, and children. Now there is only mother, father, and sometimes a single child. Families are having less influence as children are exposed to many other influences." By way of example, the superintendent described the case of a college-aged man who had murdered his parents: after two unsuccessful attempts to get into the college of his choice, he became a *rōnin* (the term literally means "masterless samurai"), that is, a student who spends extra years preparing on his own in the hope of passing the entrance examination to a university. In the course of studying for his third attempt at the Waseda University examination, he was reprimanded by his father for drinking and stealing money. The twenty-year-old student retaliated by bludgeoning his parents to death with a metal baseball bat. In an editorial on the incident, *The Japan Times* noted the excessive pressures experienced by the *rōnin,* and another "characteristically Japanese element," namely, "that the parents were victims of credentialism, obsessed with the notion that their son must go to a well-known university."[3]

Another aspect of juvenile delinquency reported by this officer was that, "Historically, delinquents came from poor families, but increasingly they are drawn from the middle class, as in the case of shoplifters."

Talking with the young chief of the Motofuji police station in Tokyo concerning the controversy surrounding the *kōban* system and whether it should be dismantled, he said that it was dangerous to generalize because situations differ throughout the country— there are residential areas, urban districts, entertainment sections, etc. "The factor of size alone shouldn't be the exclusive determining factor—regions change and evolve. Decisions on increasing or decreasing *kōban* should be dealt with on a case-by-case basis."

Concerning the possible need to centralize manpower to handle problems of traffic control, criminal investigation, and delinquency in schools, he responded, "There's a need to take into consideration not just police perceptions, but the proven fact that the *kōban* system acts as an effective pipeline of communication that has strong implications for crime control and juvenile delinquency." The chief cited as an example of cooperation between police and citizens in his jurisdiction the use of "walking patrols"—citizens, both with and without police, patrolling the neighborhood. The December holiday season typically involved a rash of house break-ins, and crime prevention block-watch groups had apparently reduced the incidence of this during that time.

Concluding the discussion of the *kōban,* he offered an illustration of a different approach. Kanagawa Prefecture had experienced rapid population increases, but due to financial constraints, combined with the need to occasionally mobilize significant numbers of men, it was decided to use a mobile *kōban,* a police box operation that works out of a large van.

Concerning future problems facing the police, he mentioned disaster and crisis relief associated with earthquakes. He felt that the need to coordinate all municipal services, including fire, was a challenging one. One wrap-up session with a police inspector at the Seijō station yielded this analysis: "It's primarily based on population, and there are plans to switch personnel more often instead of keeping them in one post for such long periods. Also, we're considering increasing the number of patrol cars throughout the district—to that extent it's a move toward centralization." The inspector reported that Shinjuku (a large shopping and entertainment section of Tokyo) had solved the problem of increasing manpower in one of its own areas by establishing a "mammoth" *kōban*. As suggested by the name, this type of *kōban* has more manpower assigned to it than the average police box.

Despite the problems mentioned above, in general the Japanese police seem to find fulfillment in their work. Relatively good police–community relations, a highly organized system of benefits and promotion, and the lack of violence in Japanese society all contribute to making police work a desirable profession.

NOTES
1. Walter L. Ames, *Police and Community in Japan* (Berkeley, California: University of California Press, 1981), p. 165.
2. William Ouchi, *Theory Z: How American Business Can Meet the Japanese Challenge* (New York, N.Y.: Avon, 1981), p. 27.
3. *The Japan Times*, "Lessons from the Tragedy," December 1, 1980, Editorial page.

Chapter 7

CRISIS WITH YOUTH

Overview

The term "crisis" is a strong one, but there has been a rapid statistical increase in juvenile delinquency in Japan, and the situation is perceived as a crisis by many Japanese. Some of these young people are taking to motorcycles in groups, called in Japanese *bōsōzoku*, literally, "rough running tribe," reminiscent of America's "Hell's Angels," while others are on the rampage in the classroom, assaulting teachers and fellow students. The underlying causes of this rising delinquency appear impervious to a quick solution. Superficially, the lack of direction and sense of purpose of many young Japanese people resembles the problem in the United States, but in Japan it is directly tied to the pressure-cooker atmosphere in schools, where the competition is almost unbearably intense. Success in Japan, as has been mentioned, is a matter of having attended the right schools. In the highly materialistic society of the eighties, there is every indication that the level of competition and its unfortunate corollary, juvenile delinquency, will continue to be problematic for the Japanese.

While statistics tell only part of the story, they are worth examining. As with adult crime, it is not easy to draw comparisons between the United States and Japan, especially since the two countries have different legal definitions of juvenile delinquency. In the United States, authorities define juvenile violators as those under eighteen years of age, while in Japan those under twenty are considered juveniles. I have used the Japanese definition and adjusted

United States data accordingly to facilitate comparisons. For the most serious crimes such as murder, arson, robbery, and rape, during 1979 the Japanese Ministry of Justice reported 2,104 offenses by those under twenty years of age, while United States authorities (U.S. Department of Justice, 1980) reported a staggering 85,042 crimes for the same age bracket. In the same year, for the less serious crime of theft (including offenses such as shoplifting, picking pockets, and bicycle theft), 146,469 offenses by juveniles were recorded in Japan, while United States authorities recorded 584,236 offenses. These figures for Japan, a country with ten million students in junior and senior high schools, are quite low, and there is no question that the problem of juvenile delinquency is much greater in the United States, but it is the rapid rise in offenses in Japan that alarms National Police Agency experts and scholars.

A frequently cited cause for the rise in juvenile delinquency in the United States, at least until recent years, has been a simple demographic one: the juvenile population was rising and there were thus more young people to get in trouble. This argument, however, does not help to explain the Japanese case. Japan's juvenile population has remained relatively stable through the past three decades, and actually declined from 38 million in 1950 to 35 million in 1978.

Another phenomenon is common to both countries, however, and it is one that many observers consider even more alarming than the overall increase in juvenile crime; that is, the growing number of very young offenders, increasingly junior high and even elementary school age.

The Japanese view the rise with concern. They fear that traditional values, especially those of cooperation and group action, are being threatened by growing individuality:

> The greater the degree to which a society respects individual freedom, the less the power of groups to control individual behavior. The root cause of present-day delinquency in Japan may well lie in the quickly weakening ability on the part of adults to exercise constructive influences on children through families, schools, and communities.[1]

This alarm is echoed in newspaper editorials, and by probation officers, juvenile counselors, and National Police Agency personnel charged with administering juvenile offender programs.

Bōsōzoku

While the source of various juvenile crimes may be similar—parental discord, weakening family ties, and the self-indulgence of young people—the symptoms vary. At least one manifestation, the *bōsōzoku* motorcycle gangs, has little to do with the creeping individuality feared by the authorities. The members of these groups are not seeking individual expression but a sense of belonging that their society has taught them to need, yet refused to grant them. The bikers are generally disaffected youth seeking the interpersonal rewards of membership in one of the few places they can find it. As one biker put it, "When we ride together, we feel we are together."

Bōsōzoku members, as individuals, do not demonstrate a strong sense of self, but are far more assertive in groups, according to a number of psychologists and scholars. K. Hagihara, a psychologist who has worked extensively with juvenile offenders explained that, at a Juvenile Classification Home, "Even in the case of motorcycle gang members, when you are observing them individually, they are quite obedient, passive, and polite. Surprisingly, they are occasionally university students. They don't have their own ego, but seek identity through gang behavior."

This analysis can be extended to most juvenile offenders. The typical juvenile offender, in Hagihara's opinion, has changed over the years and now reflects a dependent personality. Hagihara claimed that offenders over a recent five-year period have been indulged by their parents and are consequently immature for their age. Often, they have a sense of being "defeated," particularly by the education system.

A study of these groups conducted in the mid-seventies by Tamura and Mugishima (1975) found that eighty-five percent of the members were under twenty years of age, with the majority, fifty-two percent, being from blue-collar families. Forty percent were in junior high school, thirty-one percent had dropped out of high school, and just twenty-eight percent had graduated from high school. Most were described as middle-class youths who lacked hobbies or outside interests with the exception of motorcycles or cars. In comparison with other non-delinquent youth, their lack of educational achievement was the most salient feature. Membership in *bōsōzoku* gangs was rather short-term, averaging from six months to one year. These usually well organized groups varied in size, with approximately half of them being composed of about thirty members, approximately one-third between thirty-one and one hundred members, and approximately one-fifth more than one hundred members.

The *bōsōzoku*, or "hot rodders," as one official called them, resemble American motorcycle gangs:

> They dress in peg pants and black leather jackets; they are into German Army helmets and Nazi swastikas. They stomp all over traditional (Japanese) values of order, discipline, and decency. "Being bad is a badge of honor," says "Black Emperor" Masato Momose, sixteen. "It makes me feel strong, like I'm a man."[2]

Their crimes are also similar to those of their United States models. An official of the delinquency section of the National Police Agency provided the figures on *bōsōzoku* given in Table 7.

Breaking these totals down, he noted that while offenses were most commonly traffic violations, they also included gang fights, rapes, and serious crimes associated with the use of motorcycles and other vehicles. While there was an apparent curbing of these

Table 7
Number of *Bōsōzoku* Groups and Members

Year	Groups of *bōsōzoku*	Individual members
1977	365	24,322
1978	307	22,442
1979	381	19,643
1980	835	35,151

crimes in 1979, as a result of an amendment to the traffic control law that allowed for arrest on the charge of reckless driving in groups, the rate jumped again in 1980.

Incidents involving young "toughs" make headlines in the newspapers. *The Mainichi Daily News*,[3] an English-language daily, reported the case of four young men and a woman between the ages of eighteen and twenty-one who attacked a police officer in Nagoya. Sergeant Takashi Kawamura, on bicycle patrol, observed a car running a light. The car cut off the officer and he was shouted at by the occupants—"you fool," "idiot," and so on. The car's occupants allegedly beat him with his club and hurled saké bottles at him. Claiming to be fearful for his life when the youngsters tried to drag him to a nearby parking lot, he fired one shot into the air as a warning and three at the youths, injuring two of them. Claiming that the officer warned the youths, police officials initially said his actions were justified as a case of self-defense. Later, however, police officials in Aichi Prefecture decided to have the the public prosecutors conduct further investigations.

However, this case is extraordinary. As of November 18, 1980, there had been just seventeen cases in which police had shot and injured civilians since 1976.[4] This statistic helps to make clear the fact that, by at least one measure, police brutality does not appear to be a major factor in triggering the rising rate of juvenile crime. In fact, many activities of the police, including centers and hot lines, may be helping to control the problem. A poll conducted by the Prime Minister's Office found that citizens feel that the police should crack down on *bōsōzoku*, although they generally gave a good rating for police performance.

Young Offenders

Police handled 1,558 cases of school violence in 1980, up 29 percent from the previous year.[5] Of those cases, 1,202 occurred at junior high schools, while the remainder were at senior high schools. Police arrested or took into custody 798 students charged with beating or injuring 532 teachers during 1980. This represented a 69.8 percent increase from the previous year. One National Police Agency official was quoted as saying, "Some students in the past did hurl abuse at their teachers but did not go beyond that. They are now armed with bamboo swords and baseball bats. School violence involving teachers has never been more rampant."[6] Another official declared, "It's increasingly vicious; they're using steel pipes and knives now."

The fierce competition in schools and the pressure it creates have resulted in violence in the classroom (*kōnai bōryoku*) and at home (*kanai bōryoku*). Unable to deal with the oppressive atmosphere, young people lash out at those around them. Besides violence, there is escapism: drug offenses among school students, particularly the use of stimulants, are not uncommon despite strict drug laws.

The Japanese are perhaps even more troubled by what they perceive to be the underlying causes of these problems. Most Japanese do not consider the pressures of their society to be the problem, but rather the increasing inability to force individuals to submit to those pressures. The blame for increasing juvenile delinquency is divided between family and school. One study by a Japanese social scientist (Uchiyama, 1979) found that delinquency-prone primary school children appear to be those who are frequently left by the parents to fend for themselves. In a survey of 1,174 non-delinquents and 172 delinquents, 50.4 percent of delinquents compared to just 19.8 percent of the non-delinquents claimed to have visited department stores with friends (as opposed to parents), of frequented "game centers" with peers (33.3 percent delinquents, 14.8 percent non-delinquents), suggesting a lack of supervision. The researcher reconfirmed the common assumption that delinquents are more often from broken families and lower socioeconomic strata than non-delinquents. The Japanese *White Paper on Youth* for 1981 reported that 72.8 percent of the parents of delinquents took it for granted that they should leave their off-spring "unleashed."

A conversation with Professor Aiba, a former probation officer who currently teaches courses concerned with the problems of juvenile delinquency at a college in Hokkaido, supported some of these views. She said that her own youngsters were thirteen and fourteen years of age and that they frequently informed her of what was happening in their school. Typically, she said, there would be a minor precipitating factor. The offending youngsters would take another child to a lavatory area and "hit and kick" him. She viewed it as a kind of scapegoating in response to the intense pressure of school, and felt that educational competition had increased in the past ten years and that the hierarchical ranking of both secondary schools and universities was even more sharply perceived. This increased pressure, combined with a "low frustration tolerance" due to excessively indulgent parents, results in juvenile çrime. When I asked her if problems with juveniles foreshadowed increases in adult crime, she strongly protested. "It's true that Japanese people love their children and indulge them, but we don't think they will be cold-blooded. The main fault is indulging them, not neglecting them." As mentioned previously, not everyone agrees.

Like other scholars and criminal justice professionals with whom I talked, she was convinced that if teachers were stricter, violence in schools could be reduced. At a conference of teachers held in Tokyo in January 1981, there was considerable discussion on the role of teachers in curbing delinquency in the school:

> At these schools still harassed by disorder and lack of discipline, the numbers are said to be rising of teachers who seek refuge in the teachers' room as soon as class is over and those who "see, hear and speak no evil" and, therefore, do nothing about the situation that calls for their most serious attention.[7]

Besides this apparent apathy on the part of some teachers, there is also a lack of professionals to deal with the problem. Professor Aiba noted that schools in the Sapporo area had very few counselors and school psychologists and that, unlike the situation in the United States, there were practically no psychotherapists (either psychiatrists or psychologists) available to offer treatment.

My own visits to several junior high schools resulted in one particularly illuminating comment from an administrator in Sapporo: "The big problem psychologically is that they feel they have no purpose for the future. Some have no idea what they wish to do occupationally."

At times, this lack of direction and the frustration it entails result in attacks on parents, teachers, and classmates, but it is also directed inward, in many cases contributing to Japan's extremely high rate of suicide among the young. This rate is thirty percent higher than in the United States and on the average, two people under twenty years of age commit suicide daily in Japan. A breakdown by age of all officially determined suicides is given in the next chapter.

One rather extensive study by Hoshi found differences between delinquents and non-delinquents in the perception of family interpersonal relationships, which are so vital to socialization in Japan. Some of the specific findings gathered from groups of 213 delinquents and 279 non-delinquents were:

1. Delinquents perceived themselves as having longer periods of time at home on weekdays but less frequent involvement with parents on weekends and holidays than their counterparts.

2. Relationships with both mother and father were perceived more negatively by offenders.

3. Delinquents perceived more conflict in parental relations than did non-delinquents.

4. Delinquents perceived their mothers as disciplinary agents more often than fathers.[8]

Juvenile Counseling Centers

As a counseling psychologist who once worked with federal offenders in a pre-release counseling center, often called a halfway house, in Brooklyn, New York, I was particularly interested in learning about Japan's Juvenile Counseling Centers. I made arrangements to visit the headquarters of the M.P.D. counseling service in the Kasumigaseki section of Tokyo and four branches in Shinjuku, Setagaya, Sugamo, and Asakusa. There were seven centers operated by the M.P.D. in 1980. Some prefectural and municipal police agencies in other parts of Japan also offer counseling services for juveniles, but the M.P.D.'s operation is the most elaborate. In addition to counseling centers operated under the auspices of police agencies, 548 Juvenile Guidance Centers were administered by cities, towns, and villages throughout Japan during 1978 (National Statement of Japan, 1980). Among the counseling services offered by police, which often prove to be the first step in referring a problem, were the hot lines, or crisis lines, that have been established at sixty-one police stations throughout Japan in recent years. In 1978, these "Young Telephone Corners," as they are called, provided assistance to 88,343 persons, 29,474 of whom were juveniles, while 58,869 were parents or other adults (National Statement of Japan, 1980).

Interviewing the director of the "Young Telephone Corner" in Tokyo, I was informed that the service started in 1972 with a great deal of publicity. It is the only one in Japan that operates twenty-four hours a day. Information and the center's telephone number are disseminated mainly through the schools, but it is frequently parents who call, and the problem most often has to do with a crime that has already been committed. The parents are generally upset and seeking advice. Calls from young people are generally not about suicide or other life-threatening situations, but more often involve family or school problems. The staff member I observed at Tokyo's "Young Telephone Corner" had at least seven years of street experience in working with juveniles. There were seven staff members, two of whom were civilians who had degrees in psychology while the others were out-of-uniform police officers. No doctoral level psychologists or psychiatrists were involved in this operation. Asked about trends in the calls, the director remarked that there had been a slight increase in calls related to family violence. Like most counseling services, referrals were made to other agencies when it was deemed appropriate, as, for example, in the case of medical or sexual problems.

The director of the M.P.D. Juvenile Counseling Centers explained that 53 percent of the persons served by the centers came directly for help; most were parents, with just 1 or 2 percent being juveniles. Other than these persons, referrals to the counseling centers during 1979 included: 11.2 percent by police officers; 1.5 percent by civilian volunteers; 8.2 percent by schoolteachers;

4.3 percent by the "Young Telephone Corner," and 7.2 percent by private persons.

A manual for staff members entitled "Techniques of Counseling" illustrated the approach that is used. At the outset the manual cautioned, "Counselors do not make a record of smoking or drinking violations or of two people riding on a motorcycle" (technically, all of the above are illegal for people under twenty). The manual went on to encourage an emotional involvement with the client as opposed to a "businesslike" approach, but it added that since counseling has a lot to do with the relationship between human beings, the counselor should be personally secure and offer an objective point of view, a statement that might appear in any American text on counseling.

The headquarters was staffed with eight counselors, six of whom were police officers, and other branches also had a mixture of police officers and civilians. Each Juvenile Counseling Center served four or five police stations. Shinjuku personnel indicated that their main function was to go into the streets of the Shinjuku area (a particularly popular entertainment district) to offer guidance to youth. These activities would include observing youngsters who were loitering, frequenting "game centers," or drinking and smoking. Often, civilian volunteers join the plainclothes police on these patrols. The police assigned to this duty include both male and female officers.

I accompanied some of these staff members early one afternoon. They were quite easily able to identify youths in the above categories, and of course during school hours the presence of minors is particularly noticeable. By engaging them in informal conversation, the officers try to learn whether a youngster is a runaway. If they confirm that he is, they will hold the youngster until he is picked up by a parent or guardian. In cases where there is a potential danger to the young person in releasing him to the parent, the staff member might recommend family counseling. As long as the minor has not broken the criminal code, the service must be offered strictly on a voluntary basis. As in the United States, the biggest problem confronting the counselor is that those persons—parents and children alike—who are in the greatest need of help are the ones least likely to seek it.

When family members do become involved in counseling, they usually come once or twice a week for six months. One family that came to the Shinjuku center had been coming for over six years. One counselor noted that most youngsters they encounter are not bona fide runaways, but are merely "hanging around."

A growing self-interest on the part of both parents and children was often pointed out by staff members as a problem. During a discussion with counselors at the Sugamo center, one of the staff made the following observation:

> Earlier, if a boy was taken into custody, other members of his group would come to inquire, but today, with greater individuality, the peer group is less supportive. Superficially, there is group membership, as in dress, but young people don't form such close bonds.

Another, older counselor spoke of the erosion of parental authority:

> The authority of the father is declining. Even if one of his children is acting badly, the father seems unable to act. The mother is more reluctant than she used to be to firmly direct and supervise the education of the child. She seems more willing to shift this responsibility. It's not always that she seeks more time for herself, but that she is somehow less conscious of her responsibilities. Most importantly, the parents are so concerned with the academic credentials of their children that they neglect to develop relationships with their offspring.

An average caseload for each of the two counselors at the Sugamo center was 120 cases per month. The other ten personnel attached to this center were all police officers who went out in the streets offering guidance and giving "cautions." "Cautions" are not recorded and therefore have no legal ramifications.

I sat in on a number of counseling sessions at the Asakusa center. The program was started in 1963, and the staff seemed proud of the fact that their's was the first branch to be established.

One case involved a thirteen-year-old junior high school student who refused to attend school. He frequently fought with his friends and visited "game centers," returning home late at night. Though he had six sisters living at home, his counselor was convinced that he received little attention from family members: "the mother could not recall ever having caressed the boy."

Observing the session between this boy and his counselor, I was impressed with the rapport she had established. Despite cultural differences, I readily sensed the warmth and empathy this woman exuded. After ten minutes of conversation, she left for a few moments and returned with some big chunks of clay. As they each started to shape the material, they talked. The boy mentioned that he would be attending a residential school in Shizuoka Prefecture, but he said that he would still like to come every day and visit her. When the boy mentioned that he had been thinking of saving his money, the counselor supported this idea, saying, "Yes, that is better than spending it at 'game centers.'" The boy's behavior toward the counselor resembled that of a child toward its mother, and I was struck by his apparent docility.

The counselor inquired, "How is your father? Does he hit you?" To which the child responded, "No." The counselor said, "Perhaps it is because you are behaving better." The session continued with a discussion of his relationship with his friends and his frequent school absences. At the end of the session, the boy asked whether he could visit her the next day, but the counselor scheduled him for the following week. The youngster had received counseling six times at ten-day intervals. The counselor had no professional training, but she did have thirty-two years of experience working with juveniles. She noted that the boy was typical of many that were counseled at the Asakusa center: "not relating well at home or at school, timid, and with underlying feelings of inferiority."

Another case involved several members of a family with severe financial problems. The couple had married when the wife was eighteen and worked in a cabaret. The husband made a cash payment for her release from employment. The marriage had started stably, but after a number of years the woman began to drink, and marital fights followed. She eventually attempted suicide, and a year after the attempt, she died in an apparently accidental fire that destroyed the family home. It was believed to have been started by her cigarette.

Of the children raised in this environment, the elder of the two daughters was sixteen and had graduated from junior high school, but was unemployed and often spent the night with her boyfriend. The other sister, at fourteen, seemed to be influenced by her elder sister and had recently stayed away from home for a week. The son, thirteen years of age, had joined a group of *bōsōzoku* and spent most of his time riding his motorcycle. At school, he was physically violent with his classmates and often yelled at his teachers, although he seemed responsive to the supervision of one of them.

While sexually promiscuous young women occasionally receive counseling at the Juvenile Counseling Centers, prostitutes in Japan are usually over twenty years old, and thus do not fall under the juvenile code.

Conclusion

Japanese officials now refer to the recent upsurge in juvenile crime as the "third postwar peak" (National Statement of Japan, 1980). They link the first peak, around 1951, with the social unrest and economic deprivation that followed Japan's defeat. The second peak, around 1964, was the period in which large numbers of young Japanese migrated from rural to urban areas to seek employment in heavy industry. The growth of urbanization brought in its wake major changes in social, economic, and family institutions. The current wave of juvenile delinquency appears to be linked to the emergence of affluence and its consequences: educational pressures, lack of parental nurturing, the growth of individualism, and the erosion of traditional family values. Any number of scholars and police personnel have pointed to the lack of purpose and "self-indulgence" of Japanese youth. But Japanese society has not, as yet, developed a tolerance for self-indulgence, and those who cannot "fit in" experience despair, the symptoms of which have been identified in this chapter. One major symptom of underlying depression and low self-esteem is drug abuse, a subject to be covered in the next chapter. In addition to the Juvenile Counseling Centers, the Family Counseling Office plays a major role in the disposition of juvenile cases. The treatment of juvenile offenders is handled by probation officers, halfway houses, Juvenile Counseling Centers and a variety of juvenile residential institutions. The role of the Family Counseling Office and of related programs is discussed in Chapter 8.

NOTES
1. National Statement of Japan, *Crime Prevention and the Quality of Life*. Statement prepared for the Sixth United Nations Congress on the Prevention of Crime and the Treatment of Offenders, 1980, p. 23.
2. *Newsweek*, "Japanese Graffiti," October 12, 1981, p. 58.
3. *The Mainichi Daily News*, "Four Young Toughs Shot by Policeman," November 18, 1980, p. 1.
4. *The Japan Times*, "Policeman May Be Prosecuted for Shooting Youths in Scuffle," November 18, 1980, p. 2.
5. *The Japan Times*, "Anti-School Violence Drive To Be Launched," January 23, 1981, p. 2.
6. *The Japan Times*, "Schools, Local Police Told to Stem Violence," January 28, 1981, p. 2.
7. *The Japan Times*, "Testimony on School Violence," January 17, 1981, p. 12.
8. E. Hoshi, "Parent–Child Relations and Parental Discipline in Delinquents' Families: A Comparative Study between Delinquents and Non-Delinquents on Perceived Interpersonal Relations within the Family," *Reports of the National Research Institute of Police Science*, Volume 19, 1, September 1978.

Chapter 8

FAMILY COUNSELING, DRUG ABUSE, AND CRIME PREVENTION

Family Counseling

Komarigoto sōdan (trouble consultation) is the term the Japanese use for the counseling, both formal and informal, offered to citizens by the police. This counseling is closely linked to crime prevention, both in the theory and practice of the Japanese police. As noted earlier, crime prevention in Japanese police operations enjoys a divisional status equal to "patrol" and "criminal investigation" (see Fig. 3). United States police agencies have not organized crime prevention services into separate units, reflecting the fact that crime prevention by police is not a well-developed concept in the Unites States and perhaps not even a priority for police administrators. By contrast, in Japan, officers in the Crime Prevention Division engage in a variety of duties, which are described in the latter part of this chapter. Not least of these is the *komarigoto sōdan*, which I would like to consider first by virtue of its differences from what are normally thought of as crime prevention activities.

In addition to crime prevention officers who offer counseling, each of Tokyo's ninety-five police stations has a "family affairs" staff person assigned to it. The "family affairs" officers and crime prevention personnel usually counsel citizens who bring their problems to the police station. However, a considerable amount of informal counseling is also done by patrol officers at the *kōban*. An official of the Tokyo Family Counseling Office, an arm of the Tokyo Metropolitan Police Department, stated that forty-eight percent of all counseling cases were handled directly by *kōban* personnel.

Before discussing the specific forms of counseling offered by police, a word seems in order about how the Japanese generally view counseling and its more sophisticated cousin, psychotherapy. Dr. Haruo Akimoto, Director of Tokyo Metropolitan Matsuzawa (Psychiatric) Hospital, reported that only twenty or thirty psychiatrists are in private practice in Tokyo and not more than one hundred in all of Japan. Furthermore, conversations with other Japanese psychologists brought out the fact that some of those psychiatrists were probably not psychotherapists (offering verbal, or "talk," therapy) but were medication-oriented practitioners. Apparently, psychotherapy is not fashionable among the Japanese, despite their marked tendency to emulate most other Western crazes. There seems to be no history of seeking relief from emotional problems through seeing psychiatrists, social workers, or psychologists. No police officer, either in the United States or in Japan, would pretend to offer formal psychotherapy, but counseling on family or personal problems, as practiced in the United States, clearly bears a relationship to the more sophisticated treatment offered by professional psychiatrists.

Trained as a professional counseling psychologist, I was particularly interested in the counseling offered by police. When I asked about the training of officers who did counseling, including those at the Family Counseling Office, I invariably received a puzzled look. In Japan there is apparently no special training for this work. Let me add quickly that this is not meant as a criticism of their work but reflects the lack of formal preparation for personnel at all levels of counseling. Counseling by police personnel in some cases seemed to have a therapeutic component, but it often served merely to mediate a dispute.

As in the United States, police are asked to intervene in domestic or family disputes. Despite the availability and convenience of an emergency telephone line, Japanese family members are still reluctant to call for police assistance when trouble breaks out, although officers report a gradual change in this attitude. One patrol sergeant at a Seijō *kōban* commented on the incidence of "family fight" calls in his jurisdiction, an upper-middle-class neighborhood:

> Family fights for this *kōban* area average one every two weeks, and far more often than not (perhaps ten to one) we deal with this problem at people's homes, as opposed to their coming in. Before we had the emergency telephone system—perhaps twenty-five years ago—people were reporting fights far less frequently than now. Also, a feeling of shame was a bigger factor twenty-five years ago. People were more reluctant to call in the police. Values have changed, and there is greater concern for one's rights.

In addition to mediating in family fights, Japanese police counsel citizens on financial, civil, and neighborhood matters more than American police do. While professional counseling as indicated above is fairly rare, there is in its place a long history of the police officer working as a helpful mediator in disputes.

As the chief of the Motofuji police station in Tokyo observed, "Husband–wife problems are sometimes resolved by the third party who had arranged the marriage, and when people do come to the police, they do not usually come for advice on matters of divorce or sex." Two examples were mentioned as being typical of problems brought to the station for police assistance: 1. A mother came in worried about her daughter. They had moved to a new residence and disputes had erupted in the building. This seemed related to the fact that they had received a very cool reception from the neighbors; 2. A conflict over payment of rent between a landlord and tenants flared. Tenants refused to pay the recently raised monthly rent and the owner responded by shutting off the water. All parties were called and the police helped to settle the matter. (The chief added that most people are still reluctant to bring such problems to court and that this is also a reflection of the low level of legal awareness on the part of the Japanese people.)

Police policy makers view the handling of family problems as possibly preventing more serious acts and even criminal offenses, and strongly encourage officers to be helpful to citizens with these concerns. The existence of Juvenile Counseling Centers, along with the Tokyo Family Counseling Office of the M.P.D., offers concrete evidence of their concern for this problem. The *Police White Paper* of 1980 stresses the importance of police "listening to troubles attentively." This is in marked contrast with the policies and attitudes of many United States police departments.

Having personally tried to promote "crisis intervention" training for police in both the United States and Canada for more than a dozen years as a psychologist and criminal justice educator, I have had a great deal of exposure to police attitudes on this subject. Many individual police officers as well as administrators and policy makers regard family disputes as non-police work that they are required to do because social agencies cannot handle it or are not available twenty-four hours a day. Despite the fact that twenty-two percent of all police officers who have lost their lives in recent years have done so while intervening in domestic disputes (Parker and Meier, 1975), American police departments still provide little training to handle these potentially explosive situations. The comments of individual American officers range from "I answer the call and get the hell out as fast as I can" to "I can't spend time on these calls to help people because my sergeant is on the radio telling me to get back on the street." Whether it is a reflection of insecurity about this ability to handle people who are emotionally upset or because departmental priorities place other problem areas ahead of domestic crisis intervention, the result is the same—American police are very reluctant participants in these encounters. Of course, the physical hazard cannot be discounted in explaining this reluctance.

The Japanese *Police White Paper* provides data on the growth of *komarigoto sōdan* and a breakdown of the types of problems serviced. In 1975 there were 146,067 instances of assistance offered by police. This number increased steadily to 179,433 in 1979. The types of problems handled by police are presented in Table 8. The *White Paper* also gives the age and occupation of those assisted by police personnel (Tables 9 and 10).

The coordinating agency for the counseling work of the police is the Tokyo Family Counseling Office, which is next-door to the headquarters of the Juvenile Counseling Center in the Kasumigaseki

Table 8
Komarigoto Sōdan ("Trouble Counseling")
(1979; total: 179,433)

Family problems		"Civil" matters		Crime prevention		Miscellaneous	
"One's personal life" 27,528	(15.3%)	Financial 13,693	(7.6%)	Crime prevention related 23,185	(13.9%)	Miscellaneous 21,175	(11.8%)
Divorce matters 7,640	(4.3%)	Property 10,773	(6.0%)	Other 39,610	(22.0%)		
Dependents 2,501	(1.4%)	Different types of contracts 11,327	(6.3%)				
"Poverty" 1,706	(0.9%)	Other 4,741	(2.7%)				
Other 15,554	(8.7%)						
Total	30.6%	Total	22.6%	Total	35.0%	Total	11.8%

Source: *Police White Paper* (National Police Agency of Japan, 1980).

Table 9
Komarigoto Sōdan ("Trouble Counseling")
(1979; by age)

Age range	Percentage
Under 20	2.9%
20s	17.4%
30s	25.2%
40s	23.7%
50s	17.9%
60 and over	12.9%

Source: *Police White Paper, op. cit.*

Table 10
Komarigoto Sōdan ("Trouble Counseling")
(1979; by occupation)

Occupation	Percentage
Lower level salary workers	19.7%
Salary workers	25.2%
Company executives	2.4%
Managers	3.9%
"Independent" workers	20.0%
Housewives	22.1%
Unemployed	15.0%
Laborers	7.5%
Others	10.2%

Source: *Police White Paper, op. cit.*

Table 11

Japanese Suicide Rate

(1979; per 100,000 persons of the same age)

Age range	Total			Male			Female		
	Number	%	Rate	Number	%	Rate	Number	%	Rate
0–9	4	0.0	0.0	3	0.0	0.0	1	0.0	0.0
10–14	89	0.4	1.0	62	0.5	1.4	27	0.3	0.6
15–19	826	3.8	10.2	579	4.3	14.0	247	3.1	6.3
Total: Youth	919	4.2	2.6	644	4.8	3.5	275	3.4	1.6
20–29	3,654	17.0	20.8	2,477	18.5	28.0	1,177	14.5	13.5
30–39	3,808	17.7	19.5	2,599	19.4	26.6	1,209	14.9	12.4
40–49	3,796	17.7	23.3	2,690	20.1	33.0	1,106	13.6	13.6
50–59	2,977	13.8	23.9	1,850	13.8	31.8	1,127	13.9	17.0
60–64	1,164	5.4	26.9	650	4.9	34.1	514	6.3	21.3
65 and over	4,999	23.3	48.5	2,320	17.3	52.9	2,679	33.0	45.2
Total: Adult	20,398								
Not Identified	186	0.9	—	156	1.2	—	30	0.4	—

Source: *Police White Paper, op. cit.*

section of Tokyo. The administrator with whom I spoke proudly announced that the office had been in existence since 1920, and had counseled over two million people. She told me that in one-third of the ninety-five police stations under the M.P.D.'s jurisdiction, special rooms were being set aside to provide space for counseling. In 1979, 33,555 cases were handled by family counseling staff. Of these, 2,000 were counseled by this central office, while the remainder were served by the ninety-five family affairs officers and crime prevention personnel at outlying stations. People came to the Family Counseling Office in response to referrals from police officers, advertising, and word of mouth.

Suicide

The total number of officially identified suicides in Japan for 1979 was 21,503 (Table 11). This number does not include suicides "covered up" by embarrassed family members, a practice common both in Japan and the United States.

Noteworthy is the fact that of those under nineteen, many more are males (644) than females (275). This disproportionate rate of male suicide extends up through the working years with males in the thirty- to fifty-year category committing suicide at more than double the rate for females. One can only surmise that the work setting is a major factor contributing to this phenomenon. As more Japanese women find jobs outside the home, this ratio may change.

Japanese authorities have gathered data on "reasons" for suicide, apparently from notes left by the deceased, or even from interviews with family and friends. The most common reason given is "suffering from illness/disease," which was cited in 9,599 cases (44.6 percent). One suspects that many of these are older persons. The second most common reason is what is termed "emotionally upset/alcoholic symptoms," accounting for 3,708 (17.3 percent) cases. Many of these may perhaps be attributed to the above-mentioned stress of the workplace. Next were "family troubles" with 2,234 cases (10.4 percent). Suicide related to "schooling" accounted for 366 cases (1.7 percent), which, though relatively low in the context of all suicides in Japan, is, as mentioned earlier, high when compared with the data for American youth.

Table 12

Adult Runaways/Missing Persons (69,635)

(1979; by occupation)

Occupation	Total
"Average" salary workers	13,796
Executives	322
Managers	135
Housewives	12,164
Factory workers	7,445
Employees: entertainment business	3,936
Managers: entertainment business	893
Day laborers	3,757
"Independent" workers	3,120
Private businessmen	941
Salesmen	698
Unemployed	18,400
Others	4,028

Source: *Police White Paper, op. cit.*

Table 13

Runaways/Missing Persons (100,051)

(1979; by age)

Age	Total	0–9	10–19	20–29	30–39	40–49	50–59	60
Number of runaways	100,051	764	43,307	23,272	17,277	8,630	3,331	3,470
Percentage	100.0	0.8	43.3	23.3	17.3	8.6	3.3	3.4

Source: *Police White Paper, op. cit.*

Runaways and Missing Persons

The problem of runaways and missing persons is one that concerns both uniformed police and counseling staff. For purposes of statistical analysis, "runaways" are not distinguished from "missing persons." In 1979 there were 100,051 runaways/missing persons in Japan, a decline of 966 from the previous year, but substantially above the total of 91,845 runaways recorded during 1975. For 1979, there were 5,151 more adult female than adult male runaways, many being housewives (see Table 12). Reasons for running away included "love affairs and marriage problems" and "family troubles." These were by far the most frequently given reasons (30.1 percent). Seventy percent of those who ran away because of "love affairs and marriage problems" were women. Forty percent of those were in their twenties, about thirty percent in their thirties, and about thirty percent were teenagers. As the age of runaways increases, emotional problems or disease become more frequently offered reasons. Table 13 shows that the largest percentage of runaways are teenagers (43.4 percent), with the number declining steadily to reach a low in the "over sixty" age group. Teenagers' most frequently given reasons for running away include "dislike of school" and "being rebuked by parents."

The number of runaways found has increased since 1975 with over 15,156 being located by 1979. Approximately fifty-three percent returned home by themselves, the police made contact with twenty percent, and citizens were involved in six percent of the cases. Most of those who left their families or spouses returned safely, but 2,663 (2.5 percent) had committed criminal offenses, 1,567 (1.5 percent) had committed suicide, and 809 (0.8 percent) had become victims of crime.

A social scientist at the National Research Institute of Police Science, Kanehiro Hoshino, has looked beneath the surface of the statistical data to obtain a clearer picture of this problem of "running away," and some of his findings point to a cycle of despair, exploitation, and eventual suicide. In two different studies conducted during 1972, he drew on samples of 130 offenders who had left home and 761 randomly selected family members from among those who had consulted the police. Runaways came from upper-middle, middle, and lower classes. Family relationships were characterized as lacking mutual understanding, with little cohesion and with little effort being made by family members to help each other in instances of occupational failures or illness. Often the families of runaways seemed indifferent and failed to file missing person reports. Often those who left home and became offenders lacked formal schooling. They also had a history of violating the law, with almost half of them being ex-convicts.

Four and four-tenths percent of the runaways themselves became victims of exploitation, and Hoshino draws a depressing picture of their fate. They were often young women who left home impulsively. Consequently, they relied on strangers such as *tehai-shi* (owners or employees of illegal employment agencies) to find employment. As a result of their status, they were easily exploited directly as prostitutes or as hostesses in bars and cabarets, where prostitution is an "open secret." Hoshino explains that *tehai-shi* often rape these women to force them into prostitution, and also insure that they will not return home, for fear of bringing disgrace to their families.

Police acknowledge that prostitution exists but appear to close their eyes to it. Only in recent years was it declared illegal, and officers complain that the cover of the Turkish baths, the principal outlet, makes it difficult to apprehend violators. In one conversation, an officer confided that he knew some single officers who enjoyed visiting Turkish baths during off-duty hours. Data on prostitution, gathered by social scientists at the National Research Institute of Police Science indicated that the average age of Turkish bath prostitutes is twenty to twenty-two years, while "streetwalkers" tended to be a little older. Furthermore, the former group have better incomes and appear to exercise more choice in deciding to engage in prostitution (i.e., they seemed attracted to it rather than forced into it by economic hardship). For example, Turkish bath prostitutes gave the following reasons: "to get much more money for their future life" and "to get a high standard of living," but streetwalkers cited "poverty," "broken home," and "running away from home."[1] The researchers concluded that

Turkish bath prostitutes were drawn to this way of life for the income, while social conditions appeared to be a factor in encouraging streetwalkers to take up prostitution.

Running away sometimes preceded suicide or what superficially appeared to be accidental death. Researcher Hoshino stated that "many suicides are erroneously treated as persons who accidentally died." This assumption was made by family members who felt that runaways left home because of family conflicts or emotional problems. Also, many accidental deaths remained unidentified for one year, on the average, because family members had not reported the runaways missing.

Data on drunks, lost children, and the emotionally disturbed are taken from the 1980 *Police White Paper*. While most drunks are not arrested in Japan, if a person is endangering himself or others, or damaging property, he can be taken into custody. During 1979, 123,000 persons were detained for the above-mentioned reasons while 2,202 persons were referred to the health center on suspicion of being alcoholics. Aside from drunks, 145,018 other individuals, of which more than half were children, were taken into protective custody.

The Drug Problem

The problem of drug abuse in Japan is quite different from that in the United States. Stimulants, which are the major cause of concern in Japan, rank low on American authorities' list of priorities, but there is no denying that drug abuse is a major crime problem in both countries.

Claiming that narcotics-trafficking is America's most serious crime problem, U.S. Attorney General William French Smith announced a reorganization of federal law enforcement agencies in an effort to improve the nation's ability to combat this problem. For years, F.B.I. Director J. Edgar Hoover managed to stay clear of involving his agency in drug enforcement, fearing that his agents might be corrupted by the large amounts of cash associated with drug deals. However, the size of the problem grew immensely during recent decades, and United States officials decided that placing the Drug Enforcement Administration under the F.B.I. would strengthen drug enforcement efforts. To what extent this strategy has succeeded is unclear.

Japan, as an island nation, has an advantage when it comes to controlling the importation of illegal drugs, but the abuse of domestic substances, such as paint thinner, by juveniles is not easily curtailed. A study of 552 teenage stimulant users conducted by the National Police Agency in 1981 found that seventy percent had been questioned and reprimanded by police on more than one occasion. Two-thirds of the group had experimented with sniffing paint thinner. Many of the males said that they paid for their drugs from earnings, and most of the females claimed that prostitution supported their habit. Some teenage women noted that drugs were provided free by the gangsters with whom they were living. In July 1980, the National Police Agency reported that arrests of stimulant users was twenty-six times what it had been ten years earlier.

The World Health Organization (WHO) used the term "dependence" in defining addictive drugs. A dependence-inducing drug, by their definition, is one that creates a strong desire in the user to take the drug regularly either for the experience or to avoid the pain of its absence. Psychological dependence is formed initially, followed by physical dependence. Eight dependence-inducing drugs are named by WHO, but opium, cocaine, and stimulants are considered a particular problem because addiction is powerful and rapid. In addition, certain drugs have a resistance or immunity characteristic that requires the user to increase the dosage to obtain the same effects.

The appeal of stimulants is linked to their immediate, powerful effect on healthy adults. The user feels free from fatigue, excited, and there is an increase of confidence. Addicts often spend large amounts of money to support their habit, and as in the United States, this often leads to criminal behavior. Stimulants act quickly on the nervous system, but often their effects linger for years and include "flashbacks." During the period from 1947 to 1957, 146 addicts were hospitalized in Tokyo, and of that group, 23 were still hospitalized in August 1959, 15 of whom still complained of "flashbacks."

The History of Drug Abuse

The poppy plant, used in the manufacture of opium, is said to have been introduced into Japan during the Muromachi period (1333–1568) and was used for medicinal purposes from the mid-Edo period, or around 1750. Tight control was maintained and violators were sentenced to death. The severity of punishment, along with Japan's isolation, served to limit the amount of drug abuse. Later, during the Meiji era (1868–1912), the government had learned the lesson of the Opium War and developed a strict policy toward abuse and trafficking.[2]

Japan remained relatively free of drug abuse until the post–Second World War period. Statistics indicate that approximately 100 people were arrested annually on drug charges until 1930. The number jumped to around 600 in 1935 but then declined.

From 1945 to 1955, stimulant abuse was widespread. From 1955 to 1965, heroin and sleeping pill abuse by juveniles increased. After 1965, the use of paint thinner and hemp and a second peak in stimulant use were recorded. From 1945 until 1965 stimulants were manufactured in quantity and sold to a market that included soldiers, students, entertainers, and writers. They were sold as "pills to remove fatigue." The Stimulant Drugs Control Act of 1951 was enacted in an attempt to control this problem, and prohibited the importation, manufacture, selling, buying, possession, and abuse of stimulants. The law resulted in illicit manufacture and distribution.

The peak year was 1954, when 55,664 persons were arrested under the Stimulant Drugs Control Act. Potential abusers were estimated at 550,000, with 200,000 suffering from emotional disturbance as a result of addiction, while 2 million persons were estimated to have used the substance. As it became evident that the Stimulant Drugs Control Act was only marginally effective, the criminal penalties were increased in 1954, and a legal requirement of hospitalization for addicts was added. The law was further expanded in 1955, and law enforcement authorities, supported by citizen groups, had some success in reducing the manufacture of these illegal substances.

Heroin began to replace stimulants in 1955, and its use spread rapidly from 1957. The demand for heroin increased as that for Philopon (benzedrine, the most common stimulant) was declining and gangsters sought new ways to generate funds. The concentration on drug-trafficking was due in part to the enactment of the Prostitution Prevention Law, which limited their income in that sphere. Chinese sellers developed an international smuggling network in cooperation with Japanese organized crime, and heroin was sold rather openly on the docks of Kobe, Yokohama, and other port cities. In a move similar to that directed at stimulant abusers, legal penalties were increased in 1963, and hospitalization was made compulsory for heroin addicts. With the support of citizen groups, abuse declined a few years later.

Japanese authorities say that the smoking of hemp started around 1960 and became somewhat fashionable in imitation of use by foreigners. Just 1,041 persons were arrested in 1979, of which 76.8 percent were under thirty years of age. Most hemp was imported, mainly, according to police officials, from Southeast Asian countries and the United States.

Stimulant Abuse

By 1969, modest declines were observed in most forms of drug abuse, but after 1970 there was another rapid increase in stimulant abuse. Survey research by Nakasato and Tamura (1974) found that twenty percent of stimulant abusers had ties to gangs, while fifty percent were members of such gangs themselves. Their research involved samples of delinquent boys, high school students, and university students. These subjects had little history of abusing other drugs and claimed to have acquired knowledge of the substances through TV and weekly magazines.

The decline of traditional moral values and the growth of a pleasure-seeking ethic contributed to this second upswing in stimulant abuse. In 1978, among crimes for which the offender was jailed, stimulant-related crimes (approximately 12,000) ranked second to burglaries (16,000). Gangster groups once again were prominent in the business. For example, Osaka police arrested members of the Shokaizan group in the early seventies and seized

280 kilograms (616 pounds) of stimulants that had been channeled through Switzerland. For 1982, the National Police Agency reported that 2,750 juveniles were apprehended for stimulant abuse, a rise of 6.8 percent from 1981.

Due to the high price of stimulants, juveniles resort to paint thinner more often than adults, who rely more often on hemp. Users, asked why they could not stop their drug habits, gave the following reasons, ranked by frequency: "because of friends," "good for sex," "good for illness and pain," "because of night work," and "I'm addicted."[3]

Two brief sketches of juveniles who became addicted were offered in the 1980 *Police White Paper*:

Case 1
In Kyoto, a group of eight high school boys was encouraged to try stimulants by a gangster who said, "If you inject it, you'll feel so refreshed that it will make your hair stand on end." They became addicted after one year. One relied on insurance money from a brother who had died in a traffic accident, secretly withdrawing it from the bank without his parents' permission.

Case 2
In Chiba Prefecture, nine high school girls no longer received pleasure from paint thinner which they had been abusing, so they obtained stimulants from a gangster group which was led by a member of *bōsōzoku*. They took stimulants in motels and engaged in sex with gang members.[4]

Relating stimulant abuse to occupation reveals that blue-collar workers engaged in construction and public works projects are the most frequent abusers, followed by members of the service trades (restaurant, bar, and cabaret workers), and then by workers in small businesses. In the last few years, an increase in use by housewives is particularly noteworthy. Truck drivers and taxi drivers who are drug abusers have come to the attention of police because of accidents in which they have been involved. In one case, a thirty-five-year-old taxi driver in Fukuoka smuggled stimulants to his fellow workers, saying, "These are good for keeping you awake and getting over fatigue." Of the 120 employees, about 30 were taking stimulants in their locker rooms and radio dispatch rooms during working hours.

Drug Control in the Future

Alarmed by the high rate of drug abuse, particularly of stimulants, government agencies, including the Prime Minister's Office, are involved in a major effort to solve this problem. One line of attack is the widespread media campaign to educate Japanese youth and adults about the hazards of stimulant abuse. These efforts frequently include use of print media and television. Local governmental officials have joined the Prime Minister's Office in publicizing the risks posed by the use of these substances. Counseling offices operated by police have participated in the campaign, along with the telephone "hot line" services referred to earlier. Japanese law enforcement authorities have continued to pursue vigorously their drug enforcement efforts as they believe that European approaches, which conceive of drug abuse as a disease and thus stress medical treatment, have failed to control the problem.

Crime Prevention at the National Level

Various features of crime prevention have been described elsewhere, but the topic deserves to be examined in terms of the way services are integrated and how crime prevention operates within the Japanese police system. While traditionally neighborhood associations were active in crime prevention work (see the earlier discussion of *chōnaikai* and *burakukai*), the multilayered crime prevention associations of contemporary Japan are more sophisticated and highly organized. While Japanese police agencies make major contributions to crime prevention, much of the work is done by volunteers at the community level. Ames's point is well taken that crime prevention should be considered as just one of the ways in which Japanese have historically engaged in voluntary community service:

> Volunteerism covers a wide range of areas, from voluntary

welfare-case workers (*minseiin*) and voluntary probation officers (*hogoshi*) to the myriad of citizen support groups that surround the police. Similar types of persons are engaged in all the various volunteer activities, and often the same persons hold several positions simultaneously in different voluntary service organizations. They are mostly elderly men, often over sixty, and usually they either are self-employed shop or small-factory owners or are retired. Unlike office or factory workers, they have free time to spare for engaging in community service activities.[5]

Uehara, one of the administrators of Crime Prevention at the National Police Agency was helpful to me not only in providing a thorough briefing on crime prevention activities in Japan, but in arranging numerous visits to crime prevention associations (*bōhan kyōkai*) and the counseling services discussed earlier in this chapter. Superintendent Uehara noted that as of 1980, there were 1,200 associations throughout the nation. While the associations work closely with police, members are strictly unpaid volunteers. The police agencies maintain a liaison through their own crime prevention officers. The contact points for crime prevention work at the grass roots level are the "Crime Prevention Information Centers," as the 1980 *Police White Paper* calls them. These centers are referred to as "liaison posts" and are found in supermarkets, newsstands, and private homes. Each post is represented by one person and, astonishingly, there were 660,000 in 1979, which is approximately one post for every fifty-four households.

Nonetheless, even with this extremely impressive organizational network, the National Police Agency plans to re-evaluate and strengthen its work in this field. Due to weakening traditional social controls, police officials express alarm about the future:

> As a result of turmoil in the social-economic environment, local communities have been seriously eroded, anonymity increasingly characterizes modern life, pleasure-seeking trends are increasing and traditional crime deterrence in the society is waning. We fear that the crime situation in our nation will face a major change in the future.[6]

Returning to the discussion of citizen crime prevention associations, each has its chief, who works with crime prevention personnel at his local police station. Differences in strategy or other problems are negotiated between the chief and the police representative. To encourage the work of these citizen groups, police provide them with information that is relevant to their local concerns and also provide training for the leaders.

A national crime prevention campaign is held annually. In 1979 it ran from October 11 through October 20. Prefectures also plan their own campaigns, usually in the spring of each year. The elected head of a prefectural crime prevention group is apt to be a head of a bank or some other prominent citizen in the area. The theme for the national crime prevention campaign of 1979 was "Preventing House Theft and Bicycle Stealing." There were parades and speeches, popular Japanese entertainment personalities were seen on television, and posters endorsed the week's activities.

The deputy director of the National Crime Prevention Association, Akiyoshi Tsuboi, told me that crime prevention week was first held in 1964. The deputy director, a former police official, said that the purpose of his private agency was to coordinate prefectural-level association work, engage in fund raising, and assist in the shaping of crime prevention policies at lower levels. Disbursement of funds from the national office are for specific purposes such as poster campaigns, purchase of radio or television time, or the publication and distribution of pamphlets. Approximately twenty to thirty percent of the total funding for a local grass roots association comes from the national office, with the bulk coming from prefectural agencies. I asked him what he felt were the most effective approaches to crime prevention. Though he first claimed that it was difficult to judge, he then proceeded to outline a number of projects:

1. A weekly national crime prevention association newspaper.
2. An annual award based on crime reduction in a local community, which would include an evaluation of the activity level of the local group and consultation with the appropriate prefectural agency.

3. An award from the Emperor—a very prestigious award given to an individual and offered only every ten years or so.

Not surprisingly, local associations in smaller, traditional, middle-class neighborhoods are stronger than those in larger, more transient communities. Crime prevention authorities are mindful of the role that housewives play, and actively encourage their participation. In contrast, some sections of Tokyo or other large cities such as Osaka have neighborhoods with weak social networks. Areas where associations are weak are, as previously mentioned, those with a rapid turnover, usually of young couples who live in the increasing number of high-rise apartment complexes. Wealthier Japanese neighborhoods, such as those in the Seijō police station area, also have weaker neighborhood crime prevention networks. A visit to that neighborhood and conversations with several home owners reminded me of life in an affluent suburban American community, especially with respect to the loose neighborhood ties.

The work with local associations is not the only concern of national crime prevention policy makers. They are also wisely interested in city planning and the architectural design of large-scale condominiums and skyscrapers. They express concern about the increasing number of hallways and "dead end" areas in these complexes that do little to discourage crime. In planning future malls, underground parking facilities, parks, and other projects, policy makers are taking into account surveys of citizen concerns. One study completed in 1978 by Tokyo's M.P.D. found that of 2,300 women surveyed, 26.8 percent expressed concern about "few lights, and houses on streets with few pedestrians." Almost as many (23.1 percent) said they were concerned about "strange men often found in the area." The infrequent sighting of a policeman and the absence of a nearby kōban were mentioned by 15.9 percent, while a rape in the neighborhood had aroused fear in 13.3 percent of the women surveyed. Police try to respond to these concerns, and crime prevention associations have worked with other neighborhood groups to have more street lights installed.

Crime Prevention at the Local Level

Visits to local crime prevention associations yielded interesting information on activities at the grass roots level. In the Tokyo Metropolitan Police Department, individual specialists at each of the ninety-five stations receive direction and guidance on policy matters from the central office. Increased funding can be diverted into certain areas if the need arises. During 1980, a number of "model" areas received extra funding due to higher crime rates, according to Mr. Naguma of Tokyo's Crime Prevention Bureau. While acknowledging the difficulty in demonstrating a cause and effect relationship, Naguma pointed to the fact that one "model" area had witnessed a thirty percent drop in crime from the previous year, while two other areas had reported declines of ten percent each.

These supplemental funds might pay for extra house alarms, the establishment of a new liaison post, a bulletin board, or additional pamphlets and posters. Tokyo had 111,000 liaison posts in 1980. They distributed their own monthly magazine to 19,000 subscribers at a cost of ¥100 (about 50 cents) each.

Local crime prevention association members I met at the Manseibashi police station in Tokyo during the fall of 1980 said that breaking and entering and the defacing of walls were the two major concerns at that time. The members were older businessmen who lived in this busy commercial neighborhood. I asked about their activities to combat these problems. Mr. Tsuchida, their president, offered a brief history of the focus of their work over the years.

> Working with this group for over thirty years, I've seen changes in the pattern of activities. We were stimulated to establish this association right after the Second World War, when crime was high. Mainly, we patrolled the streets. Later, in the early 1970s, there were many leftists and students causing problems and we again emphasized walking patrols. Usually, we offer crime prevention information (e.g., on locks) to residents, shop owners, and others—there are 1,200 buildings

to cover, including many shops and businesses, within this jurisdiction. As members, we sometimes help police officers out on "big" cases by using community contacts. Sometimes we bring in snacks to officers required to work long hours on a particular case. Also, I should mention that we try to encourage citizens to report crimes immediately.

Another member of the association remarked that professional criminals were usually the culprits in the most recent rash of breaking and entering.

Members of a local crime prevention association in Kobe, in the central part of Japan, voiced concern about the activities of gangsters. This older port city, which had a population of 1,361,000 in 1975, has traditionally been a center of gangster activity, with the Yamaguchi group being the most infamous. The spokesman and most of his fellow members were older men, averaging perhaps sixty years of age. A perspective was offered by the Shinto priest who was their leader.

Having lived here for forty years, I've experienced Kobe before, during, and after the war. I have many citizens who come to my shrine, and they tell me what's on their minds. Organized crime is concentrated here, with 34 gangs with 880 members operating in the heart of Kobe. There are 117 groups and approximately 3,480 individual gangsters in all of Hyō-go Prefecture. They concentrate mainly on gambling, loan sharking, prostitution, and drugs. It is difficult to dislodge them because they are clever and have legitimate businesses as a front.

Association members also described their general activities. They emphasized that their main function is to provide police with information on all forms of criminal activity in their area—drug-selling, suspicious individuals, fights, etc. The Shinto priest echoed the earlier statement of a police officer when he said, "We want to be the eyes and ears of the community."

There are many bars, cabarets, and nightclubs sandwiched together in this highly commercialized center of Kobe. "Game

Table 14
Crime Prevention Approaches/Selected Commercial Establishments, 1979

Commercial establishments	Banks	Mutual financing banks	Credit banks	Credit associations	Agricultural associations	Fishermen's Union	Post offices	Others	Total
Number of facilities	8,728	3,668	5,498	2,469	16,499	2,189	21,873	3,225	64,149
Emergency bell	97.3%	97.7%	91.3%	70.2%	16.4%	6.3%	9.1%	23.7%	38.1%
TV monitor	32.0%	6.4%	9.5%	2.2%	0.4%	0.1%	0.1%	0.9%	5.8%
Camera	65.7%	36.5%	38.0%	18.4%	3.2%	0.1%	0.4%	5.1%	16.2%
Screens on counter	11.5%	3.4%	3.3%	3.4%	4.6%	8.6%	51.1%	2.9%	21.2%

Source: *Police White Paper, op. cit.*

centers," amusement parlors, and pornography vending machines attract junior high school children. As in the Juvenile Counseling Centers in Tokyo, police officers and volunteers collaborate to offer "guidance" to juveniles. One man, who was retired, coordinated the work of 100 adult volunteers who would seek out youngsters frequenting these establishments. "We approach them rather sensitively and softly, informing them that this is not the place for them, and we try to persuade them to avoid future visits. We don't wish to embarrass them publicly, but if these young people repeatedly return to these places, the police will be advised. This might result in a plainclothes officer bringing a youngster to a *kōban*, where a card will be filled out and his parents contacted."

Crime prevention was a major topic of conversation with the chief of the Motofuji police station during my field research in Tokyo. He noted that in addition to offering crime prevention information to citizens and counseling to families, crime prevention officers take custody of lost children, the emotionally disturbed, and the senile. In the case of an emotionally disturbed person, the station might receive an emergency call and, after taking the person into protective custody for twenty-four hours, refer the person to a psychiatric hospital. Though these procedures are effective in removing the individual from an environment in which he might do harm to himself or others, there was some concern among legal scholars about the broad authority of police to detain and hospitalize mentally ill persons.

"Trying to assist individual citizens in ways that actually prevent crime and working extensively with crime prevention associations are the two major objectives of the crime prevention section," the Motofuji chief observed. He outlined some of his future concerns:

> It's true that the transiency of people in neighborhoods, along with the growth of individuality as an attitude toward life, has decreased the willingness of people to report crimes, but it means we must try to build even stronger cooperation among citizens. It means an even greater expansion of the service aspects of policing. An example of how this pays off is

the case of a taxi driver who helped solve a murder. The taxi driver came forth with some critical information, and it was accidentally discovered that he had previously been helped by a police officer. The driver claimed that he had been so impressed by the assistance offered to him that it had contributed to his desire to help police on this homicide case.

Other Areas of Crime Prevention

Recently, there has been significant growth in the private security field. The first company was established in 1962, and the number of security guard firms increased from 1,682 in 1975 to 2,622 in 1979, while the number of guards rose from 71,333 to 104,765 (*Police White Paper*, 1980). The work of these firms includes security at nuclear power plants, the transportation of large amounts of money, and guard work at construction sites. During 1979, 13,145 persons were arrested through the cooperation of private security personnel. As in many Western nations, security operations in the commercial sector, including banks and financial institutions, rely increasingly on technological and mechanical devices, such as TV monitors, emergency alarms, and cameras, to prevent crime. A survey conducted in December of 1979 detailed the types of protection various commercial institutions have employed in order to prevent crime (see Table 14).

NOTES
1. Y. Takahashi, H. Nishimura, and S. Suzuki, "A Social Psychological Study on Prostitution (II): The Comparison between the Streetwalker and the Turkish Bath Prostitute," *Reports of the National Research Institute of Police Science*, Volume 16, 2, December, 1975, p. 97.
2. This section relies on the *Police White Paper* (National Police Agency of Japan, 1980) unless otherwise noted.
3. *Ibid.*, p. 34.
4. *Ibid.*, p. 29.
5. Walter L. Ames, *Police and Community in Japan* (Berkeley, California: University of California Press, 1981), p. 41.
6. *Police White Paper, op. cit.*, p. 77.

Chapter 9

THE POLICE AND THE COMMUNITY

Public Opinion Surveys

One way to obtain a sense of the relationship between the police and the community is to examine public opinion surveys. In 1968, researchers at the National Research Institute of Police Science (Nishimura and Matsumoto, 1968) surveyed 478 people in Tokyo. One of their most interesting findings concerned responses to the question, "Do you have any fear of policemen?" While just 19 people said "very much," 112 indicated an in-between, or "average," rating, and 197 said "very slight," Another 128 responded "not at all." Not included in the analysis were 17 responses. Among those surveyed, teenagers had the most negative and uncooperative attitude, while white-collar workers and owners of small businesses were the most positive and cooperative.

Additional information has been provided by surveys conducted by the Prime Minister's Office. Table 15 provides a breakdown of data from adults gathered during 1972 and 1979. The striking similarity between the data reported in 1972 and 1979 suggests the consistently positive attitude that citizens have toward the police. One suspects that Americans would not be nearly as generous. The figures show what any observer can easily feel: that the Japanese do not view their police as enemies—a situation all too common in the United States. Nonetheless, as has been suggested elsewhere in this book, there does seem to be a trend in the early eighties toward an increasing distance and a weakening of social bonds between the police and citizens. This change can

Table 15

Prime Minister's Office Survey on Attitudes toward Police
"Do you feel friendly toward the *kōban* policemen?"

Random samples
1972: 1,044 adults (over 20)
1979: 996 adults (over 20)

	1972	1979
1. Friendly	40%	39.4%
2. Somewhat friendly	45%	43.2%
3. Not friendly	7%	7.4%
4. Don't know	8%	10 %

be seen in some of the interviews described earlier, and just a hint of it is in evidence in the large-scale survey data, especially that on fear of the police.

In a discussion with Hoshino about his research he said, "There is widespread trust in and respect for the police, but generally citizens do not wish to be close to them." He continued:

> There are discrepancies in the attitudes of citizens toward the police. For example, for minor offenders, such as a "Peeping Tom," people want an arrest, but police will usually only give a warning. Another discrepancy might be the enforcement of an election law violation. Citizens would permit this violation, but the police do not. Of course, citizens are not always happy with the strict enforcement of traffic laws, but the police usually enforce them consistently, provided the manpower is available. Generally, the public believes that the police do not rigorously enforce laws with regard to top-level managers, politicians, and others. They gain support for their views from the Japanese press.

Fujiwara (1980) reported on a 1974 newspaper survey of one thousand citizens concerning the politicizing of police. Thirty percent of the respondents felt that the police were "neutral," or not political, twenty-seven percent indicated an "average" category, while thirty-eight percent felt the police were political. Five percent said they didn't know.

In a major study of citizens' attitudes toward crime, Hoshino prepared a series of interrelated papers, published as *Reports of the National Research Institute of Police Science* (1975, 1976, and 1977). The program surveyed 8,160 citizens in 350 communities (with 329 police stations) and found that the fear of crime is significantly related to the closeness of the relationship between police and citizens. Not surprisingly, in communities where citizens perceive a closer relationship, there is more reporting of crime, and citizens thought more police patrols, detectives, and police boxes contributed to a reduced fear of crime. In discussing his research, Hoshino noted that a closer relationship between police and citizens not only affected fear of crime, but could be related to lower crime rates as well. To what extent this relationship actually reduces crime is unclear, but a correlation does seem to exist. Also, there was a positive effect on the crime rate when the policemen who work in a community live there. Hoshino has also studied the correlation between various fears (e.g., of earthquake, power failure) and found that fear of crime is independent of other fears.

A study of foot patrols was conducted in Newark, New Jersey (Wilson and Kelling, 1982), and it was found that residents of the neighborhoods patrolled on foot felt more secure than persons in other areas. They tended to believe that crime had been reduced and seemed to take fewer steps to protect themselves (e.g., "staying at home with the doors locked"). While Wilson and Kelling admit that actual crime rates appear not to have been reduced as a result of the experimental foot patrols, they point out that the order-keeping behavior of police helped to create a better quality of neighborhood life, since officers were able to act as a control on drunks, derelicts, and suspicious-looking strangers. Sometimes the officers were enforcing the law, but just as often they were "taking informed or extralegal steps to help protect what the neighborhood had decided was the appropriate level of public order."

The authors argue convincingly that the order-keeping function of police (and citizen groups), which has been on the wane in recent years, should be vigorously renewed in order to preserve community controls and reduce crime:

> A stable neighborhood of families who care for their homes, mind each other's children, and confidently frown on unwanted intruders can change, in a few months, to an inhospitable and frightening jungle. A piece of property is abandoned, weeds grow up, a window is smashed. Adults stop scolding rowdy children; the children, emboldened, become more rowdy. Families move out, unattached adults move in. Teenagers gather in front of the corner store. The merchant asks them to move; they refuse. Fights occur. Litter accumulates. People start drinking in front of the grocery; in time, an inebriate slumps to the sidewalk and is allowed to sleep it off. Pedestrians are approached by panhandlers. At this point, it is not inevitable that serious crime will flourish or violent attacks on strangers will occur. But many residents will think that crime, especially violent crime, is on the rise and they will modify their behavior accordingly.[1]

Wilson and Kelling point out that citizen groups (like the local crime prevention associations in Japan) can help to fill the void in maintaining public order where reduced budgets prevent a strong police presence on the streets in the form of foot patrols.

One final point of interest from Hoshino's work, which is no doubt as valid for the United States as it is for Japan, is that the perception of levels of police patrols and activities is generally lower than those that actually exist. Furthermore, citizens tend to desire a minimum level of police presence above the level that they perceive actually exists. As Hoshino explains, "If a citizen thinks there are 300 policemen in his city then he may ask for 500; if he believes there are 200 in his community he wants 300."

Comments from Scholars and Criminal Justice Professionals

Interviews, both formal and informal, with justice officials, scholars, and private citizens offered a depth of analysis that public opinion surveys lack. While I made no attempt to sample groups scientifically, the comments and thoughts of Japanese citizens helped me to understand the way the police are perceived and supplemented data from the broader surveys of public opinion.

One court official offered this evaluation of the police:

> The police have a mission to prevent crime, but the salary is not very high. They receive awards based on the number of arrests they make. For example, a special badge or certificate is awarded to those who excel. In a democratic society there is freedom of thought and expression, but in the Japanese police organization individuals are asked to be faithful and loyal to the police agency. The police have no labor unions; if an officer is sympathetic to socialism or the Communist Party, he will have to resign from police work. Freedom of expression is an impossibility within the police organization. Instead, an officer forms a close friendship with fellow policemen. The public regards an officer as a friend in a time of trouble, but if people are demonstrating, they feel that the police are against them. During demonstrations, the police occasionally arrest citizens for minor violations.

A conversation with two legal scholars at a Tokyo university yielded the following comments: "Japanese police place too much emphasis on political activities—like student radicals and demonstrations by citizens. Rather, they should focus more on common crimes, such as burglary." The second scholar stated that he had "no basic criticism of the police," but he went on to describe one instance in which he went to ask the police about a lost article. He was surprised and annoyed that they questioned him extensively about his occupation and working hours.

A criminal law professor at Kobe University echoed the earlier concern regarding police behavior on politically related matters.

> The police don't respect the rights of labor unions as much as they should, and this is also true for the public election laws. Furthermore, they don't fully back up the notion of equal protection when it comes to political parties such as the Communist Party. There are also problems with the procedures

for criminal investigation, particularly in voluntary situations where no warrant has been issued.

He offered several examples of cases that had been decided by the Japanese Supreme Court in the early eighties in which the police had gone too far, in his opinion, in manipulating and coercing witnesses into cooperating and giving self-incriminating evidence. As in the United States, there are Japanese proponents of stronger "search and seizure" laws, but there are also scholars and critics who wish to see greater safeguards for the procedural rights of citizens. In general, he felt that police officers are highly competent but "perhaps too much so." Sensitive to the legal dimension, he questioned how well low-ranking officers were trained in the law.

As in the United States, law professors frequently have a different perspective on law enforcement than do the police themselves. Scholars have the luxury of being distant from daily encounters between the police and citizens, while the police are where the action is. One dean of a Japanese law school, remarking on the "routine visits" of the police, expressed skepticism concerning their avowed purpose. While conceding that the police generally were effective in the crime prevention facet of their job during their visits to homes and commercial establishments, he was concerned about how far they might go in their desire to learn about suspicious activity in the neighborhood. This mixture of "routine visit" and not-so-routine criminal investigation would quickly raise the issues of invasion of privacy and violation of rights in the United States. One can imagine the uproar that the American Civil Liberties Union would create if the police were to make visits to all homes twice a year and, in the course of the visit, make subtle inquiries about neighborhood activity.

One former American Midwestern police officer, who enjoyed the friendship of a number of Japanese police, had somewhat mixed feelings about the police agency generally. He had resided in Japan for several years and was most familiar with officers in the Japanese *kidōtai*. Like most foreigners, he was impressed by the fact that the police are not treated as much like "outsiders" as they are in

America and that they enjoyed a strong *esprit de corps*. But he expressed annoyance at the behavior of Japanese officers who stopped him on the street.

> Relationships with foreigners are not good here. When an officer approaches me, I'm apt to be treated badly—you can get harassed easily and frequently. An officer will stop me and not say, "Hello," but rather, "Show me your passport." At least half a dozen times I've had my sword case with me and I've been stopped. When you might expect the older policemen to be indifferent, they are the most helpful.

While the "sword case" might offer some explanation for the police's behavior, the foreigner's annoyance can be attributed to the fact that Americans are generally accustomed to greater freedom of movement and expression. On the other hand, it might be interesting to know how many Americans, with escalating crime rates, might not appreciate a system in which officers are alert to unusual behavior and have the right to stop and question an individual who appears suspicious. Wisely or unwisely, we may be approaching the point where we will allow broader powers for the police to investigate crime.

A probation officer in Hyōgo Prefecture said she generally found the police effective and respected, but expressed concern over the *kidōtai*, particularly in their work with street demonstrators. "The police in the *kōban* are friendly, but the riot police are too zealous in their control of young people who are demonstrating." She felt that police practice overkill in the numbers they put on the street. "I saw fifteen or less university students walking around in the street, but more than twenty police had been mobilized."

The Views of Private Citizens

There follows a sampling of the responses of members of the general public to my inquiries about their reactions to the police.

A man in his mid-thirties whom I met by chance in a Tokyo library touched on several familiar themes:

> Before World War II, the Japanese police had a great deal of

power and they exercised it. They engaged in thought control directed primarily at socialists and communists. As a result of the U.S. Occupation, freedom of thought was introduced, and the police were reorganized after the war was over. Nowadays, Japanese police behavior appears hesitant or deferential, but as soon as they are given a reason for needing their power, they will show it. When the reason exists they become like a bear or tiger! I feel a bit fearful of the police even though I have committed no offense.

When I pressed this man for a more exact explanation of his "bit fearful," he gave the answer I had heard many times. "When I was a child, my parents said to me, 'If you misbehave, a policeman will come and catch you.' In short, Japanese citizens are frightened at the prospect of jail, and the police have the power to put them in. I cannot understand it exactly, but police are a symbol of fear."

I was introduced by a probation officer to the general secretary of a YMCA in Yokohama, and our conversation started when he offered a few historical notes. He observed that the strong hierarchical structure of imperial prewar Japan had changed under the new constitution, but the deeper authoritarian roots remained. He felt that the police reflected this shift; while officers are friendly on the surface, deep down, underneath their facade of friendliness, they are authoritarian.

People do believe that the police can maintain peace and order and that they can be relied upon. Older people perceive the police as representatives of authority and feel that they cannot resist their requests. In the countryside, the policeman was a very important person in the community historically, and is today as well. The wife continues to share some of his duties in rural locations. The officer still is very service-minded, doing counseling—he's kind of a father figure.

In the sixties, he said, police and students engaged in battles in the streets and on campuses, but the atmosphere became increasingly less political in the seventies. "Today young people are enjoying the affluent society—they're more conservative and there are few encounters between them and the police. It's a kind of benign relationship." He recalled an incident with police when he was a youngster growing up in the late 1930s:

> When I was in fourth or fifth grade, I was at home by myself. I was tending the fire for the Japanese bath when it got out of control. I yelled "fire!" and many people came to the house and helped me put it out. After my father returned from the bank (my father was an executive of a bank and highly respected), he was called to the police station. It was a very bad experience for him. He was held responsible for my behavior. His one comment was, "I was treated like a criminal. I've never felt that way before."

The adult students of an English class in Sapporo provided a wide spectrum of responses to the question, "How do you feel about police officers?"

Twenty-eight-year-old male: "When I drive and am stopped for speeding, the police are too lenient, but I generally have a good impression. They make society safer."

Twenty-six-year-old woman: "Socially Japan is orderly and it's a safe society. We have a good relationship with the police and I am proud of them."

Forty-year-old woman: "I believe the Japanese police are more sensitive than they were earlier, when I was a child. They have a friendly attitude toward children today."

Twenty-five-year-old woman: "The police don't act as strongly as they used to. Now, if you break a law, you will not be disciplined."

Older woman: "Under most circumstances the police are very reliable (for example, when I need directions), and, to tell you the truth, I feel they are kind and friendly. But inside they like having power—not physically but politically. Therefore, when I ask for help at the *kōban*, they are kind, but when I was caught for speeding, they were very rude. Thus, they change easily."

Thirty-five-year-old male: "I think the police have become

friendlier, but, as another student said, I was brought up to be afraid of the police—if I do something wrong, 'the police will catch me.' Most of us feel that there is something to be afraid of. The police have power and if possible I wish to avoid them. We need them to control crime and keep order, but I don't like policemen or their system."

Twenty-year-old female: "We can't separate the law from policemen. If citizens didn't break the law and could keep order, we would all be safe, but it is not so. I am young, and my teenage friends and I sometimes have problems—smoking, dating after midnight, driving, and so on. We're stopped sometimes, and I can't feel friendly toward the police. When my friend was driving and was stopped by an officer, he was treated harshly. The police have a strong character and they are effective—particularly in obtaining information in an investigation."

Twenty-five-year-old male: "In our daily lives the police protect us. If someone attacks me, I will immediately call for police help and receive it instantly. I am confident I will get a quick response. However, let me give you a different type of example. I have an American friend and I visited his residence which is near the Soviet Consulate. As we left his house we were stopped by the police and asked 'What are you doing here so late?' And he was asked, 'What do you have in your bag?' Another time I went to the Korean Consulate to pick up a passport and I was also asked about my purpose—the officer was fair, but it was uncomfortable. When I have been in Tokyo and asked for help or directions, I have always received excellent information and assistance."

Thirty-year-old woman: "I think the Japanese people support their police and trust them to help in an emergency such as an earthquake. They're also polite."

Twenty-two-year-old man: "I had a relative who was a policeman but who is now retired. He was very strict, but he had a tough job—he was a section chief. My opinion generally is that the police are helpful and they act friendly, but I can't trust them myself. Perhaps it's the authority. They must have authority to do the job."

Dissidents, Radicals, and the Police

During the turbulent sixties, the police and students clashed, both on campuses and in the streets. The intrusion of the police onto the Tokyo University campus was particularly noteworthy since that institution is considered preeminent in all of Japan. Visiting with a psychology professor and several of his graduate students in the fall of 1980 on the Tokyo University campus, I asked how members of the academic community viewed police involvement in these matters. It was perplexing to hear the professor begin his answer with a brief review of the history of the Japanese army. I later came to realize that this type of thinking was a holdover from the prewar period, when it was not uncommon for Japanese to associate police with members of the military establishment despite the fact that they were separate forces. Given the painful history of confrontation between students and police in the sixties, this professor noted:

> If a policeman were to walk on campus today, he would be surrounded immediately by students questioning him as to his purpose. The university has an agreement with the police department that sets down strictly the rules governing on-campus activity of the police—it must involve a serious crime and involve the pursuit of an individual offender.

While many campuses reverberated with unrest throughout Japan during this period, in particular it was the grievances of Tokyo University medical students that spawned the battles on that campus. In one incident, eighty students occupied the Central Administration Building on June 15, 1968, whereupon the president of the university called for police help. On June 17, one thousand riot police (*kidōtai*) in combat dress stormed the building only to discover that it had been evacuated by the students, who had gotten wind of the action.

The United States involvement in Vietnam was a rallying point for many students and leftists, but that faded with the end of the conflict. Brumley reported that, "Leftist radicals could muster thousands of chanting followers for military-style demonstrations and confrontations with police. But their organizations have dwindled to a few hundred that are fighting among themselves."[2] The campuses have been relatively quiet since the mid-1970s.

Two surviving factions of the student movement, the *Chūkakuha* and *Kakumaruha* groups, have engaged in a violent series of internecine battles that have raged over a number of years. In a recent chapter of their ongoing conflict, members of the *Chūkakuha* used steel pipes and hammers to beat to death members of the rival *Kakumaruha*. Police investigators claimed that the attack was so carefully planned that the assailants cut neighborhood telephone lines so that local residents were unable to phone police.

Clifford reported on similar conflicts between these rival factions in the 1970s and commented on their history. Both *Chūkakuha* and *Kakumaruha* groups are spinoffs from the earlier Unified National Committee for the Revolutionary Communist League (*Kakukyōdō*).

> *Kakukyōdō* had been founded by a group among whom were Kanichi Kuroda, the present leader of *Kakumaruha*, and Nobuyoshi Honda, former leader of *Chūkakuha*, who had been murdered by *Kakumaruha* members on March 4, 1975, at a Saitama prefecture hideout. Both groups were anti-Stalinists, revering Trotsky and Mao Tse-tung.[3]

One group claimed that there was not yet a climate for revolution, while the other group insisted on maintaining a violent revolutionary mood. Infighting continued among more than a dozen political groups during the late 1960s and early 1970s. K. Murata (1980) noted that the peak in the number of clashes was reached in 1969, when 308 were reported, during which 1,143 persons were injured and 2 were killed. Over a twelve-year period, the number of clashes ranged from about 200 in 1963 to nearly 300 in 1975, and then dropped off to 91 in 1976 and just 22 in 1979. While the number of injuries fell as incidents decreased, the number of deaths rose from 11 in 1974 to 20 in 1975. In 1976, 3 deaths were recorded and the number increased to 10 in 1977. Murata claimed that the decreasing number of incidents reflects the general decline of the power of these groups and their inability to enlist new student involvement in their cause.

Compared with the remarkably high rate of arrest in typical homicides, police have had difficulty in making arrests in these cases. The arrest rate in student battles involving deaths is only 34.9 percent, or twenty-two out of sixty-three incidents, and in the twenty-six cases involving deaths since 1976, just one arrest was made.

The role of security police increased around 1975 when Prime Minister Miki was attacked by a right-wing radical. They are now assigned to guard the current government leaders of the Liberal Democratic Party. The Japanese Red Army is also closely watched by this intelligence-gathering branch of police whose activities remain obscure not only to private citizens but to other police. There seems to be a direct correlation between the Red Army's activities and the growth of security police. This usually anonymous force gained some notoriety during the economic summit attended by President Carter in 1979, when various participants, including members of the foreign press, criticized the security as over-restrictive.

A different perspective on police behavior toward dissidents was offered by the radicals themselves, some of whom I interviewed in Hokkaido. One former Hokkaido University professor who participated in a number of demonstrations over the years, including those directed against the United States involvement in Vietnam, offered the following opinions:

Question: "Under what circumstances have you found yourself engaged in demonstrations and what was the role of the police?"
Answer: "I participated on a number of occasions in anti–Vietnam War demonstrations held around 1967. They were organized about once a month and included from ten to thirty people in the early days. I was a professor at that time. Demonstrators included students and workers; most were young people. At first, the police were friendly—just a few observed as we demonstrated with placards and a public address system. However, they always gathered information on the participants. As the demonstrations

continued, we began to hear from the police comments like, 'We know where each of you lives.'

"Certain participants, particularly younger ones, were invited by plainclothes officers to meet in coffee shops and were asked, 'What do you know about these political activities?' For the most part, people were not affiliated with organizations. I myself had to go to a police box to get a demonstration permit.

"In addition to demonstrations directed at the Vietnam War, there were also those concerning the renewal of the U.S.–Japan Security Treaty, and student protests against university administrators. Some of these demonstrations were large, involving thousands of people—perhaps half were college students. On one occasion, I received a telephone call from a police officer, and he inquired, 'How many people came to this demonstration?' But by then the demonstrators were numerous and did a French-style spreadout. The police did not prevent this, but they observed that it was illegal. At that time, one or two persons were arrested for doing a snake dance and physical contact was made. Students didn't use their hands, merely had body contact. Neither did the police use clubs; they only pushed.

"Later, when the university campus was closed, things got ugly, and both sides were more violent. Stones and Molotov cocktails were thrown, and the police responded with water canons, tear gas, and clubs. Several people were hospitalized as a result. Members of the younger generation seemed to be sympathetic to our cause, but I don't know about older people. Riot police do not react personally; they are highly disciplined. They only obey orders from their commander, and it's true that students try to provoke the police by verbal abuse.

"The dangerous aspects of police activities are not the open confrontations but rather the work of plainclothes officers working behind the scenes. Most demonstrators were anxious about the plainclothes officers. People sometimes hate them. These officers try to get the addresses of people and try to penetrate the 'new left' or other activist groups, such as those demonstrating on pollution or consumer issues. Police consider all anti-government political activity as subversive. Police are psychologically repressive, not physically repressive."

I asked the same question—"Under what circumstances have you found yourself engaged in demonstrations and what was the role of the police?"—of a student activist at Hokkaido University, at a meeting that included a law professor from the same school.

Answer: "During the past year, a number of us participated in a demonstration in front of the Korean Consulate here in Sapporo. Our activities were directed toward the release of Kim [Kim Dae Jung, a popular Korean political figure who had been sentenced to death in Korea]. About ten of us used a megaphone and directed statements at Korean Consulate personnel. We stationed ourselves about twenty meters in front of the building. About twenty policemen positioned themselves between the front gate and ourselves, but I suspect more officers were inside. Also, there were about five plainclothes detectives nearby. One of the demonstrators had the megaphone, and he was grabbed by the throat. This was after about ten minutes of having used the megaphone. His throat was held, and he was shoved on to the concrete fence, and banged his head. I don't know if it was done intentionally, but the skin was broken although there was no bleeding. I thought at that moment he might be arrested, but he was not.

"A plainclothes officer ordered all the demonstrators away from the gate, and the uniformed police pushed the demonstrators for about five meters to the side of the gate. No one was arrested. None of us resisted physically because we knew we could be arrested and that violence might erupt. Our leaders had instructed us not to give out our names or those of fellow demonstrators."

At this point, the law professor intervened with several additional comments.

It should be noted that this took place during the second demonstration and that half a dozen directed at the Korean Consulate occurred in all. On the surface, what took place might have seemed to be a violation of the Peace and Order

Maintenance Act, but this incident has to be looked at in the context of the series of demonstrations. Also, concerning the obtaining of information from demonstrators, as long as it is gathered voluntarily, without coercion, the police believe it to be legal. Of course, lawyers are skeptical of the police interpretation of the law.

The student activist offered his view of the role of the police:

The other demonstrations were non-physical, with each side acting prudently. I believe that the first principle for the police is to maintain political order as established by the governing classes. Consequently, the police act aggressively toward any anti-government activists, even if they are non-violent. Also, I believe that my fellow participants who had demonstrated for the first time were shocked by the police behavior. In the same incident I mentioned earlier, two others were shoved down by the police, and their glasses were knocked off. They had only been standing, not physically resisting.

Gun Control

Westney (1982) informs us that the Tokyo police during the early Meiji period did not carry weapons on regular duty, but from 1882 on, the right to wear a sword was extended to patrolmen as well as officers. However, the stringent restrictions on drawing the sword forced the police to rely on a less deadly weapon—the baton.

Though the Japanese police do carry guns today, the use of any weapon is very infrequent. As mentioned previously, in my own informal survey of approximately fifty Tokyo police officers, only one claimed to have drawn his weapon, and even then he had not fired it.

Tsuchiya (1980), reporting on data gathered in Japan in 1977, stated that only 5.3 percent of all homicide cases involved guns, and just 0.8 percent of robberies involved guns. In general, the Japanese have exercised far greater control over the use of firearms than Americans have.

The basic statistics on the use of guns in the United States are widely known, since newspapers and magazines review the issue frequently. A look at these statistics helps emphasize the scale of the problem in the United States. Handgun murders, which are rightfully spotlighted by gun control advocates in all countries, numbered 9,848 in the United States and 48 in Japan in 1979. There were 800 in France, 55 in Britain (excluding Northern Ireland), and only 21 in Sweden for the same year.

How do the laws themselves differ? Due to tight legal controls in Japan, only 893,000 guns and pistols of all types were owned by "properly authorized" persons as of 1979 (National Police Agency, 1980). Of authorized weapons in Japan, more than ninety percent were hunting weapons (rifles, shotguns, and air guns), which had been authorized for target shooting practice or eliminating harmful animals. These figures should be contrasted with the 55 million handguns believed to be in circulation in the United States for the same year and the estimate that about 2.5 million additional weapons would join the arsenal each year. Hunting weapons are not included in these totals.

Fewer guns translated into fewer crimes involving their use, with a total in Japan of only about 3,300 cases and the arrest of 2,200 persons during 1979 (National Police Agency, 1980). The Japanese authorities control the use of hunting weapons as well. In 1978, a "performance test" was required for each applicant to determine his skill and knowledge of the weapon. Ames (1981) found that thorough background checks are done on all applicants for a hunting weapon and that any criminal record would result in the denial of an application. He also noted that weapons had to be brought into the crime prevention section of the local police station every five years for inspection and the renewal of the permit. Furthermore, the owner was required to listen to a lecture on gun safety from the police.

The situation in the United States seems totally out of hand. In 1978, in New York City, 23,000 robberies were committed with a handgun, and over 9,000 of these weapons were confiscated by police. Though there generally are licensing or registration requirements in the United States, these are easily eluded. There are 175,000 dealers licensed by the federal government, but state laws and regulations vary. In many Southern states, no more than a driver's license is required for the identification of the buyer, and applicants are rarely checked. Thousands of guns are stolen every year, yet in New York City only 26,000 individuals have ever obtained a handgun license. Under the U.S. Gun Control Act of 1968, the major law in force as of 1982, a person who abused alcohol could not be sold a gun, yet the law again did not require a firearms dealer to investigate a buyer.

Underlying the American fascination with the gun is the notion of freedom. It seems that anybody is entitled to almost anything in the United States, with little regard for possible destructive consequences for others. America is the land where one's individual rights reign supreme, regardless of the social cost!

Research on the link between guns and aggression reported by Leonard Berkowitz (1981) indicated a definite relationship. Berkowitz and LePage found that the mere presence of guns can encourage aggressive behavior. The experiment involved 100 students at the University of Wisconsin, and its real purpose was disguised under the announced purpose of studying physiological reaction to stress. Experimental situations requiring a person to offer various shocks to subjects were used to assess the responses of the angered and humiliated "victims" to the various objects that were placed nearby. One group was not exposed to objects; a second group that had been shocked was exposed to badminton rackets and shuttlecocks; the third group was shown a twelve-gauge shotgun and a snub-nosed thirty-eight revolver. As the researchers anticipated, when subjects were allowed to return shocks (i.e., to retaliate for having been shocked), the presence of the guns affected both the number and length of time they administered shocks to their partners. A follow-up study in Sweden found that under some conditions, both non-angry and angry subjects could be equally affected by the sight of a weapon. Studies of children have found that their play activity was more aggressive when they were allowed to play with toy guns.

Organized Crime

The *yakuza* (gangsters) and *bōryokudan* (gangs) have been mentioned, but I would like to look at them more closely. I have already referred to Ames's (1981) study of organized crime in Okayama Prefecture. In addition, there is a fascinating series of studies conducted in the 1970s by Kanehiro Hoshino, Fumio Mugishima, and Ayako Tsurumi of the National Research Institute of Police Science during the 1970s that sheds light on the activities of organized crime. One of these studies, from 1973, provides a picture of *Yamaguchi-gumi* life as depicted by members of "local" and "seminational" gangs. The *Yamaguchi-gumi*, considered the most infamous and largest gang in Japan, is often compared with the Mafia in the United States. Interviews with rival gang members revealed that the *Yamaguchi-gumi* has a feudalistic class system that involves a network of 449 local groups organized in a pyramid structure. All the group bosses are subject to a single *oyabun* (head of the family). This system offers cohesiveness and a strict and arbitrary control of the behavior of individual members, who were estimated to number around 10,229 in 1973. Hoshino stated that traditional values of *giri* (obligation, duty) and *ninjō* (empathy, humaneness) are weakening, but aggression, exclusiveness, and fatalism continue to characterize major gang activities.

Pseudo-kinship relationships are still popular among Japanese gang members, and more than half of those studied maintained "brotherly" kinship ties. A ritual exchange of the saké cup in front of an altar and pledges of loyalty help cement ties. Members must obey every order of their boss. Often, a "blood oath" binds them to a code of behavior that is not easily broken. Gang members believe that this contributes to morale.

Despite the facade of honor and even patriotism (some groups have names such as Japanese Nationalist Organization, and The Great Japanese Peace Association), they are a scourge on society and drain resources much as similar groups do in the United States. It is ironic to use the term "honorable" about any group that accounted for twenty percent of all the murders in Japan during a recent year: 396 homicides were identified as gang-related by police during 1975 (Mugishima and Hoshino, 1976). The *Yamaguchi-gumi* distributes "Let's drive out drugs" leaflets, and yet gang members are often arrested for stimulant offenses. Gang members are depicted romantically in the Japanese media, but they are arrested

Table 16

Types of Crimes Committed
by Arrested *Bōryokudan* Members, 1979

Violation	Percentage
Prostitution	0.6
Dangerous weapon	0.6
Burglary	0.6
Rape	0.8
Murder	1.0
Use of poison	1.1
Entertainment Law (bars, cabarets, and nightclubs)	1.1
Interference with a government official	1.1
Destroying property	1.3
Threatening	1.4
Bicycle races, gambling	1.6
Fraud	2.2
Guns and swords	3.6
Theft	4.1
Horse Racing Law	6.5
Extortion (threat for money)	7.6
Assault	9.8
Gambling (general)	9.9
Injuring (minor)	18.5
Stimulant Law	18.3
Others	8.3

Source: *Police White Paper, op. cit.*

and convicted for such unromantic crimes as extortion and acts of violence. *The Japan Times* reported that 1,958 gang members were arrested by Tokyo Metropolitan Police in a two-month "crackdown" in the fall of 1980. In that series of arrests, forty-six handguns, eighty-nine Japanese swords, and 13.79 kilograms (about 30 pounds) of stimulant drugs were seized.

Violation of stimulant laws, discussed in Chapter 8, is a major problem in Japan and organized crime figures play a major role in trafficking. The *Police White Paper* for 1980 noted that stimulant law violations were one of the two largest categories for which *bōryokudan* members were arrested (see Table 16). The police report estimated the annual income of gangster groups at around ¥1 trillion (over $400 million). In addition to stimulant offenses, gang members were frequently arrested for gambling, extortion, and various types of assaults.

An example of how the illegal smuggling and sale of stimulants correlates with other organized criminal activity was cited by police officials:

> A thirty-six-year-old leader of a *Kaizu-Shotetsu* lineage gang group became furious with a waterworks employee who complained about the quality of stimulant he was purchasing from the leader's lover. The gangster went to the man's home with ten of his followers, took the man and his family for a car ride and threatened to kill all of them.[4]

In 1976, Mugishima and Hoshino profiled 246 murder victims of gang members from among the total of 396. More than ninety percent were male and most were in their thirties. One hundred and two victims (43.2 percent) were described as "fringe members" of the underworld, and most of the other victims were somehow tied into businesses associated with gang activity. As in the United States, some of the murders (26 percent) committed by organized crime involved complicity. In contrast to most homicides in Japan, which do not involve pistols or swords, twenty-four percent of gang murders involved pistols, eleven percent involved swords, and forty-seven percent involved knives.

In a later study (Hoshino, 1980) of 282 randomly selected gang victims, it was found that most of them were owners or employees of bars, nightclubs, construction businesses, hotels, restaurants, and loan shark operations.

In an earlier period, gang members who wished to leave their organization might suffer the loss of a finger joint or might even be lynched, but today "secession" is much easier (Hoshino, 1974). In a follow-up study of 1,713 gang members, the researcher found that approximately twenty-four percent of the members left their groups after five or six years. Many of those who left gang life were able to do so because they were involved in legitimate jobs and businesses, in addition to their illegal activities. Some were forced out of organizations due to effective law enforcement and the disbanding of their groups, while others left because of declining health or financial losses suffered at the hands of rival groups. Often those who departed were those who had conformed less to gang values even while members, and were less frequent participants in criminal activities. Approximately two-thirds of those who broke their ties with organized crime remained unemployed and/or continued to engage in illegal activities for up to four years following their departure. Semiskilled or skilled workers and craftsmen seemed particularly able to disassociate themselves completely from gang life.

NOTES
1. J. Wilson, and G. Kelling, "The Police and Neighborhood Safety," *The Atlantic Monthly*, March, 1982, pp. 29–38.
2. B. Brumley, "Japan Radical Leftists Groups Dwindle," *International Herald Tribune*, December 27–28, 1980, p. 2.
3. William Clifford, *Crime Control in Japan* (Lexington, Massachusetts: Lexington Books, 1976), p. 26.
4. *Police White Paper* (National Police Agency of Japan, 1980), p. 48.

Chapter 10

CONCLUSION

In expressing, both explicitly and implicitly, my views concerning Japanese police practices, I think I have made my very high regard for the Japanese system quite evident. Often, possibilities for learning from this system are rather obvious, and therefore I have no intention of presenting an exhaustive list of them. Furthermore, the usual caveat about vast differences in culture making some reforms impossible to achieve is eminently applicable here. Having said that, I am prepared to offer five general recommendations. Let me hasten to note, however, that while the ideas that follow are based on my research, at times I have strayed well beyond the data presented in my discussion. Moreover, I have not attempted a lengthy justification of what follows, since it is intended principally to stimulate thinking on the subject, not as a definitive solution.

The police system of the United States is much like an eight-cylinder car chugging along on six. Crime is rampant. We currently have a fragmented patchwork of inefficient, marginally trained, and poorly equipped police forces. Far too frequently, a person can become a police officer if he or she has the right political connection or a relative "in the right place." Morale is low, in part because of bickering between police managers and unions, but also because of the discouragement that talented officers feel with a system that has no mechanism to allow them to advance at a rate equal to their worth. Of all the complaints I have heard from hundreds of police officers I have taught over the past decade, none is more serious than this: it often compels intelligent, sensitive officers to leave police work. Some view a college degree in criminal justice not as a means of advancing within their police agency but as a ticket out. In too many departments there is no professional personnel system that allows the top individuals to advance. Instead, favoritism prevails. Stories abound of high-school-educated police chiefs who discourage and even harass subordinates who seek to improve themselves by obtaining college degrees. While a small number of police departments require a college degree to enter the force, most do not. In most departments, educational background has little relevance; indeed, it is not unusual to hear of a master's degree recipient taking the prescribed recruit training class alongside high school graduates.

As mentioned earlier, in Japan college-educated men and women complete a six-month course of training at the outset of their careers, while high school graduates complete a full year's course. College-educated personnel are actively sought, and currently sixty percent of police recruited in Tokyo are college graduates. The United States has no equivalent of England's Bramshill Police College or Japan's National Police Academy, which allow for upward movement based on advanced training and selection. For example, an officer in England from a local police constabulary can enter a course designed for newly appointed sergeants. After satisfactorily completing the one-year course, he can be assured of a promotion to the position of inspector. That would be virtually impossible in the United States. Nor does the United States have anything approaching the "elite" system of Japan, whereby top university graduates can enter the police field as "management trainees," with appropriate rank and salary. In Japan, riding the "fast track," they can feel assured of regular promotions and lifetime job security.

The F.B.I. Academy in Washington, D.C., in addition to training F.B.I. personnel, does offer some training courses to police officers, but its capacity is limited. Some local police departments periodically select an officer or two to attend a specialized course, but the choice of who is selected may be politically biased. The training at the F.B.I. Academy has a reputation for high professional standards, but because numbers are limited most officers never set foot inside its doors. The first recommendation is that the United States establish a national police college that would provide both advanced academic, as well as professional, training.

While it is heresy to suggest it in a nation that views its police establishment as a necessary evil, the second recommendation—a major one—is that Americans should attempt to overcome their strong emotional biases against a national police and consider at least a quasi-national system. A system that has national standards for selection, training, and promotion has many virtues, including the ability to control entrance requirements for recruits. While it would be unfair to suggest that the charges of physical abuse occasionally leveled against American officers could be eliminated by higher selection standards, I do feel that such a move would bear fruit in this sensitive area. Too few police departments adequately screen applicants according psychological criteria. Some police departments, such as those in New York City and Los Angeles, employ full-time personnel psychologists (as does the Tokyo Metropolitan Police Department), but the practice needs to be standardized. This would be facilitated by a national administration.

The need for high standards, both physical and psychological, is particularly pronounced since American officers are under much greater stress and pressure than many of their counterparts in other countries. The physical abuse mentioned above is in part a response to this, albeit that is often an excuse. Americans offer much less respect to police than do the Japanese, and the police officer–citizen relationship in the United States is complicated by racism, poor working conditions, and so on. Incidents of violence between police officers and citizens in the United States can also be attributed in part to the low level of physical fitness among American police. While Japanese police are required to maintain physical fitness through kendo or judo, it is common to see overweight, out-of-condition officers patrolling the streets in American cities. Officers who are out of shape are more insecure than those in good physical condition. Thus they are more likely to be drawn into physical confrontations with citizens. Physical and psychological standards of selection need to be tightened.

In addition to controlling intellectual, psychological, and physical standards of officers, a quasi-national system of policing would do much to remedy the current chaotic state of affairs, whereby town policing functions overlap with those of county and state police. A unified system, even just at the state level, would be more efficient and more economical. The investigation of crime would be vastly improved. Jealousies that are rampant between police and local F.B.I. offices would be greatly reduced, if not eliminated. If the public had a better image of police, the officers would in turn have higher self-esteem and would feel less pressure to "moonlight" at other jobs. Indeed, states could make it illegal, as the Japanese government does, for officers to take outside employment, thereby reducing the ineffectiveness of officers who exhaust themselves in their efforts to hold down two jobs.

This proposal for a quasi-national system, loosely linking various states, would not change the financial mechanism substantially. There would continue to be considerable autonomy in terms of funding and budgeting. In both in Japan and Great Britain, local police forces are funded up to fifty percent by local governments.

Public safety commissions staffed by local citizens could act as a buffer to control and oversee police operations. Undue political influence on the policies of these regional police forces would be minimized. The F.B.I. could either be broadened to assume a larger role in setting standards and policies for police on a national level, or a new national police agency could be created. By creating a cadre of professional police managers who could be rotated periodically throughout the different states, there would be a tremendous reduction in police corruption—which is still far too common in the United States. A professional managerial approach would supplant today's archaic police bureaucracies, where political influence rather than qualifications often determines who becomes chief. This would reduce the need for bodies such as the Knapp Commission, which was created in New York City a number of years ago to investigate widespread corruption in the police department.

I am sure that most Americans would resist the strengthening and professionalizing of the police because they fear police power, but this is, I think, a misunderstanding. Merely because police agencies would be linked to an integrated, national structure would be no reason for them to take on a strong authoritarian aspect. As in Japan, a vital unfettered press and the electronic media would serve as one of the checks on police abuse of power. Actually, in America, with its deeper democratic values, the risk of police abuse of power is even less.

We do not have to go as far as Japan or Great Britain to find a model for an integrated police force: Canada has a system that has worked effectively. With a few exceptions, such as the Ontario Provincial Police and the Quebec Provincial Police, the Royal Canadian Mounted Police (R.C.M.P.) has provided police services throughout much of Canada. There have been occasional problems in Canada's quasi-national police force, but it has been retained. Chapman (1978) sketches the historical evolution of the Canadian police and notes that as recently as 1976, eight of Canada's provinces renewed their "contracts" with the R.C.M.P. for police services. In Alberta, where I lived and trained police for two years, the force was made up entirely of R.C.M.P., with the exception of the police in Edmonton and Calgary, the two major cities. Other Canadian cities such as Montreal and Vancouver also have their own police agencies, but the R.C.M.P.'s Criminal Intelligence Service Canada has a computer-linked operation that ties in practically all of Canada's police forces. An organization such as the R.C.M.P. attracts more applicants and applicants of better quality than small, independent, local departments ever could. Occasionally, the media has alleged a scandal or abuse of authority on the part of the R.C.M.P., but for the most part corruption appears to be proportionally less among Canadian police than American.

Again, to be fair to American police officers, a Los Angeles Police Department patrol officer transferred to one of Japan's police boxes for a year, would probably undergo a dramatic change. Faced with a far less stressful environment and a much more approachable public, our American officer would become considerably more relaxed, friendlier, and helpful. The stress of urban police work in the United States might well be reduced by introducing a system of neighborhood police operations. As suggested in a previous chapter, the only movement comparable to the *kōban* system in the United States, that of increased walking patrols, has met with success, especially in restoring order to urban areas. Thus, a third recommendation, which is not new and would encounter resistance because of the high cost, would be to establish more local policing units, particularly in large cities. The Japanese example makes it apparent how important this system is, regardless of its cost, and a highly decentralized system of mini-police stations would probably be the best way to improve ties between police and citizens and thus reduce crime. Only through a national system would it be possible to implement such a revolutionary change in American police practices and to get police out of their cars and walking the beat again.

A quasi-national police system would also allow a far more effective use of manpower, and the financial benefits might make it possible to establish a greater local police patrol presence without reducing the crime fighting power of "street crime" undercover units, detectives, and so on. Manpower could be allocated according to need, with the cost spread throughout the nation proportionally. Fewer administrators, at least theoretically, would be required.

Obviously, in many small towns and rural communities in the Untied States there is a good working relationship between police and citizens. For all practical purposes, small-town policing in Japan and the United States may not be so radically different, but in municipal and state policing major beneficial changes could be accomplished. As Japan has demonstrated, it is not necessary to sacrifice a strong service-oriented police at the community level to gain an efficient national system.

A fourth recommendation would be to establish counseling centers for families and juveniles and to expand crime prevention units. Since these two services are linked I will discuss them together. While police officers in small towns currently engage in some informal counseling of citizens, most American departments shun this type of work. I feel that a change of approach in this area would help to foster a better overall relationship between police and citizens in the United States, but I also recognize that this would be a major undertaking and many American officers would argue against it.

Japan's success in crime control is due primarily to the type of society it is rather than its police force, and it would be ridiculous to predict a massive reduction in crime in the United States based on an integrated system of law enforcement of the type I am advocating. Some changes, however, could be effected, even in our very different society, with positive results. Gun control is one example and is my fifth recommendation. While a stronger federal gun control law could make a serious dent in felonious crime, without a quasi-national police force it would be difficult to implement the law.

Many features of the Japanese police system could not be transplanted easily. America's heterogeneous population, with its varied ethnic and racial groups, will never become a homogeneous society such as Japan's with its shared heritage and system of values. More accustomed to authoritarianism, the Japanese allow police to penetrate far more deeply into the community. The American Civil Liberties Union and many other organizations would be outraged if police officers started visiting every American household and commercial establishment. Traditional Japanese values of loyalty and obedience and the sense of obligation people feel for one another also contribute to the lower crime rates and help to maintain ties between police and citizens. As Japanese society continues to becomes more urban and impersonal, those values will continue to be tested. They are already being eroded. To some extent they are being replaced by the imported American values of individualism and the awareness of rights, two values that, as I have stressed throughout this work, are attacking the cohesiveness of Japanese society. The growth of juvenile delinquency in the past ten years is one of the most obvious symptoms of these weakening social controls and is the single most important crime problem that faces Japanese justice officials.

Nevertheless, though Japan's system of crime control and policing are markedly different from America's, primarily because of vast cultural differences, I am hopeful that we can take advantage of certain facets and characteristics of the Japanese system that are adaptable to our own.

BIBLIOGRAPHY

Ames, Walter L. *Police and Community in Japan*. Berkeley, California: University of California Press, 1981.

Bayley, David H. *Forces of Order: Police Behavior in Japan and the United States*. Berkeley, California: University of California Press, 1976.

Beer, Lawrence Ward. *Freedom of Expression in Japan: A Study in Comparative Law, Politics, and Society*. Tokyo and New York: Kodansha International Ltd., 1984.

Benedict, R. *The Chrysanthemum and the Sword*. Tokyo and Rutland, Vermont: Charles E. Tuttle, 1954.

Berkowitz, L. "How Guns Control Us." *Psychology Today*, June 1981.

Borchard, E. *Convicting the Innocent*. New Haven: Yale University Press, 1932.

Chapman, B. "The Canadian Police." *Police Studies*, March 1978, pp. 62–72.

Clifford, William. *Crime Control in Japan*. Lexington, Massachusetts: Lexington Books, 1976.

Dore, R. P. *City Life in Japan*. Berkeley, California: University of California Press, 1958.

————. *Shinohata: A Portrait of a Japanese Village*. New York: Pantheon Books, 1978.

Fujiwara, T. "Criminal Justice System in Japan (II): Criminal Investigation." Unpublished paper for the United Nations Asia and Far East Institute for the Prevention of Crime and Treatment of Offenders, Tokyo, Japan, fall, 1980.

Gibney, Frank. *Japan: The Fragile Superpower*. New York: W. W. Norton & Company, Inc., 1975.

Hall, J. *Japan: From Prehistory to Modern Times*. New York: Delacorte Press, 1970.

Hoshi, E. "Parent–Child Relations and Parental Discipline in Delinquents' Families: A Comparative Study between Delinquents and Non-Delinquents on Perceived Interpersonal Relations within the Family." *Reports of the National Research Institute of Police Science*, Volume 19, 1, September 1978.

Hoshino, K. "Crime, Victimization, Suicide and Accidental Death as a Result of Running Away from Home" (p. 154) and "Family Relationships and Running Away from Home" (p. 144). *Reports of the National Research Institute of Police Science*, Volume 14, 1, 1973.

––––––. "The Analysis of Descriptions of Yamaguchigumi by Members of Organized Criminal Gangs." *Reports of the National Research Institute of Police Science*, Volume 14, 1, 1973.

––––––. "Process of Secession from Organized Criminal Gangs." *Reports of the National Research Institute of Police Science*, Volume 15, 1, 1974.

––––––. "A Measurement of the Level of Public Safety from Crime (II)." *Reports of the National Research Institute of Police Science*, Volume 16, 2, 1975.

––––––. "Police Activities to Raise the Level of Public Safety from Crime." *Reports of the National Research Institute of Police Science*, Volume 17, 1, 1976.

––––––. "Police Activities to Raise the Level of Public Safety from Crime: The Satisfaction Point of Public Safety Examined by the Delphi Method." *Reports of the National Research Institute of Police Science*, Volume 18, 2, 1977.

––––––. "Victims of Organized Crime and the Process of Victimization." *Reports of the National Research Institute of Police Science*, Volume 21, 1, 1980.

Ike, N. *Japanese Politics: Patron–Client Democracy*. New York: A. Knopf, 1972.

International City Management Association. *The Municipal Yearbook*. Washington, D.C., 1980.

Ishida, T. *Heiwa no Seijigaku*. Tokyo: Iwanami, 1968.

Japan. Ministry of Justice. *White Paper on Crime (Summary), 1980*. Tokyo: Research and Training Institute, October 1980.

––––––. "Problems of Juvenile Delinquency in Japan" (Reported by Director Tabita, Juvenile Division, Criminal Affairs Bureau). Tokyo, 1980.

Japan Society, The. "The Role of Public Prosecutors in Criminal Justice: Prosecutorial Discretion in Japan and the United States." Seminar Report, *Public Affairs Series* 14, New York, September 1980.

Kanetake-Oura, B. *Fifty Years of New Japan*. London: Smith Elder & Co., 1910.

Keishichō. *Metropolitan Police Department*. Tokyo, 1980.

Kirk, D. "The Shame of Japanese Justice." *Asahi Evening News* (*London Observer Service*), February 2, 1981.

Koschmann, J. Victor. "Soft Rule and Expressive Protest." In Koschmann, J. Victor, ed., *Authority and the Individual in Japan*. Tokyo: University of Tokyo Press, 1978.

Koshi, George M. *The Japanese Legal Advisor: Crimes and Punishments*. Tokyo and Rutland, Vermont: Charles E. Tuttle, 1970.

Loftus, E. *Eyewitness Testimony*. Cambridge, Massachusetts: Harvard University Press, 1979.

McKay, R. "Japan: Streets without Crimes, Disputes without Lawyers." Unpublished manuscript, Aspen Institute Program on Justice, Society and the Individual, 1978.

Mitchell, Richard H. *Thought Control in Prewar Japan*. Ithaca, New York: Cornell University Press, 1976.

Moore, Charles A., ed. *The Japanese Mind: Essentials of Japanese Philosophy and Culture*. Honolulu: East-West Center Press, 1967.

Mugishima, F. and Hoshino, K. "A Study of Murder Committed by Members of Organized Criminal Gangs." *Reports of the National Research Institute of Police Science*, Volume 17, 2, 1976.

Murata, K. "Savage In-Fighting ('Uchigeba') among Radical Groups Goes on Relentlessly." *The Japan Times*, November 7, 1980.

Nakane, Chie. *Japanese Society*. Berkeley, California: University of California Press, 1970.

Nakasato, Y. and Tamura, M. "A Study on Stimulant Abuses in Japan and a Study on Non-Medical Use of Dangerous Drugs in Adolescents." *Reports of the National Research Institute of Police Science*, Volume 15, 1, June 1974.

National Police Agency. *National Police Academy*. Tokyo, 1980.

———. *Police White Paper*. Tokyo, 1980.

National Statement of Japan. *Crime Prevention and the Quality of Life*. Statement prepared for the Sixth United Nations Congress on the Prevention of Crime and the Treatment of Offenders, 1980.

Nishimura, H. and Matsumoto, T. "Analysis of Attitudes towards Police." *Reports of the National Research Institute of Police Science*, Volume 9, 1, 1968.

Niyekawa, A. "Authoritarianism in an Authoritarian Culture: The Case of Japan." *The International Journal of Social Psychiatry*, Vol. XII, No. 4, 1966, pp. 283-88.

Okudaira, Y. *Political Censorship in Japan from 1931 to 1945*. Unpublished manuscript, Institute of Legal Research, University of Pennsylvania, Philadelphia, 1962.

———. "Some Preparatory Notes for the Study of the Peace Preservation Law in Prewar Japan." *Annals of the Institute of Social Science*.

Tokyo: University of Tokyo Press, 1973.

Ouchi, William. *Theory Z: How American Business Can Meet the Japanese Challenge*. New York, N.Y.: Avon, 1981.

Parker, L. Craig. *Legal Psychology: Eyewitness Testimony, Jury Behavior*. Springfield, Illinois: Charles C. Thomas, 1980.

Parker, L. Craig and Meier, R. D. *Interpersonal Psychology for Law Enforcement and Corrections*. St. Paul, Minnesota: West Publishing Company, 1975.

Rokumoto, K. "Legal Problems and the Use of Law in Tokyo and London—A Preliminary Study in International Comparison." *Zeitschrift für Soziologie* 7, August 1978, pp. 228-50.

Scott-Stokes, H. "In Japan, Crime Is Rare and Reaction Swift." *The New York Times*, April 12, 1981, p. E7.

Sherman, L. *The Quality of Police Education*. San Francisco, California: Jossey-Bass, 1976.

Statistics Bureau. *Statistical Handbook of Japan*. Tokyo: Prime Minister's Office, 1980.

Sugai, S. "The Japanese Police System." In R. Ward, ed., *Five Studies in Japanese Politics*. Ann Arbor, Michigan: University of Michigan Press, Center for Japanese Studies, Occasional Papers, No. 7, 1957.

Takahashi, Y., Nishimura, H., and Suzuki, S. "A Social Psychological Study on Prostitution (II): The Comparison between the Streetwalker and the Turkish Bath Prostitute." *Reports of the National Research Institute of Police Science*, Volume 16, 2, December 1975.

Tamura, M. and Mugishima, F. "Survey on the Groups of Violent Drivers (I & II)." *Reports of the National Research Institute of Police Science*, Volume 16, 2, December 1975.

Tanaka, H., ed. *The Japanese Legal System: Introductory Cases and Materials*. Tokyo: University of Tokyo Press, 1976.

Tsuchiya, S. "Crime Trends and Crime Prevention Strategies." Unpublished paper for the United Nations Asia and Far East Institute for the Prevention of Crime and Treatment of Offenders, Tokyo, Japan, October 1980.

Uchiyama, A. "A Study On the Factors of Delinquency among Primary School Children." *Reports of the National Research Institute of Police Science*, Volume 20, 1, September 1979.

U.S. Bureau of the Census. *Statistical Abstract of the United States*. Washington, D.C.: U.S. Printing Office, 1980.

U.S. Department of Justice. *An Introduction to the National Crime Survey*. Analytic Report SD-VAD-4. Washington, D.C.: U.S. Government Printing Office, 1977.

———. *F.B.I. Uniform Crime Reports—Crime in the United States, 1978*. Washington, D.C.: U.S. Government Printing Office, 1979.

————. *F.B.I. Uniform Crime Reports—Crime in the United States, 1979.* Washington, D.C.: U.S. Government Printing Office, 1980.

————. *Criminal Victimization in the U.S.* National Crime Survey Report SD-NCS-N-18, NCJ-62993. Washington, D.C.: U.S. Government Printing Office, September 1980.

————. *Measuring Crime: Bureau of Justice Statistics Bulletin.* Washington, D.C.: U.S. Government Printing Office, February 1981.

Vogel, E. *Japan as Number One: Lessons for America.* Cambridge, Massachusetts: Harvard University Press, 1980.

Von Mehren, A., ed. *Law in Japan: The Legal Order in a Changing Society.* Cambridge, Massachusetts: Harvard University Press, 1963.

Wagatsuma, H. "Minority Status and Delinquency in Japan." In George De Vos, ed., *Socialization for Achievement: Essays on the Cultural Psychology of the Japanese.* Berkeley, California: University of California Press, 1973.

Wall, P. *Eyewitness Identification in Criminal Cases.* Springfield, Illinois: Charles C. Thomas, 1965.

Westney, E. "The Emulation of Western Organizations in Meiji Japan: The Case of Paris Prefecture Police and the Keishi-Cho." *The Journal of Japanese Studies,* 8, No. 2, 1982.

Wilson, J. *Varieties of Police Behavior.* Cambridge, Massachusetts: Harvard University Press, 1974.

Wilson, J. and Kelling, G. "The Police and Neighborhood Safety." *The Atlantic Monthly,* March 1982.

INDEX